THE FUTURE OF NEWS
An Agenda of Perspectives

Edited by

Maxwell McCombs, Amber Willard Hinsley,

Kelly Kaufhold, and Seth C. Lewis

University of Texas at Austin

Copyright © 2010 by Maxwell McCombs, Amber Willard Hinsley, Kelly Kaufhold, and Seth C. Lewis. All rights reserved. No part of this publication may be reprinted, reproduced, transmitted, or utilized in any form or by any electronic, mechanical, or other means, now known or hereafter invented, including photocopying, microfilming, and recording, or in any information retrieval system without the written permission of University Readers, Inc.

First published in the United States of America in 2010 by Cognella, a division of University Readers, Inc.

Trademark Notice: Product or corporate names may be trademarks or registered trademarks, and are used only for identification and explanation without intent to infringe.

14 13 12 11 10   1 2 3 4 5

Printed in the United States of America

ISBN: 978-1935551-84-3

www.cognella.com 800.200.3908

Contents

A Time of Turmoil — Maxwell McCombs — 1

Chapter 1
A Gutenberg Moment — David D. Brown — 3

Chapter 2
Dark Days Ahead — Kelly Kaufhold — 17

Chapter 3
Attracting Tomorrow's News Users Today — Dominic Lasorsa — 31

Chapter 4
The New Newsroom: Changing Job Roles and News Organizations — Amber Willard Hinsley and Amy Schmitz Weiss — 41

Chapter 5
Citizen Journalism: Motivations, Methods, and Momentum — Seth C. Lewis — 59

Chapter 6
Cutbacks, Countermeasures and Consequences — Brian Baresch — 77

Chapter 7
Two Other Views—Infotainment and Alternative Press — Paul Alonso and Jaime Loke — 89

Chapter 8
Social Media and News as User Experience — Cindy Royal — 107

Epilogue — 119

Contributors — 121

A Time of Turmoil

Maxwell McCombs

"You can have a Ford in any color, as long as it is black."

—Henry Ford

Henry Ford's succinct summary of consumer options for an automobile in the early days of the 20th century is a metaphoric description of our options for a daily news package across the past century. Everyone in the community received more or less the same "black Ford," a set of news articles and features that were a greatly truncated microcosm of what was happening in the world due to the constraints of the news hole and broadcast time. Now the internet has set the stage for a vastly expanded approach to news, a much broader and deeper version of the news than traditionally has been offered to the public in daily newspapers and television broadcasts. We are on the cusp of a new journalism, a journalism that will be defined by new kinds of content and new kinds of storytelling as much as by new technologies and channels of communication.

Although there are many distinctive innovative features of the internet and online journalism, such as a vastly increased level of interactivity between the public and journalists and the accessibility of internet news sources via an ever-growing host of small electronic devices, the success—some would argue, the survival—of quality journalism will hinge more on content than on the attributes of any communication medium per se. The medium is only the distribution system, and in *MediaMorphosis: Understanding New Media*, Roger Fidler noted, "People do not buy information technologies—they buy content, usefulness, and convenience at the point when they perceive value to match the cost."

In terms of content there are two key trends to consider. First, the news available to the public in the future almost certainly will be created by some coalition of professionals and ordinary citizens using a wide variety of technologies. And although the content produced by this coalition will include most, if not everything, that professional journalists have produced in past decades, the "news" in the future will be a vastly larger inventory of material than we find in today's news reports.

This supply of news for both the general public and groups with niche interests will be distributed through a vast array of outlets. Today's traditional media—newspapers, TV, and radio—are not likely to disappear, but they will be only a subset of the outlets used to access the news. The result will be a more networked and interactive system than anything that has come before in the evolution of journalism and the news media. Although the specific contours are impossible to predict, the total inventory of news will be far richer, both socially and even commercially, than its predecessors.

The eight chapters of this book delve into these trends in considerable detail and offer excellent perspective for journalists and citizens attempting to make their way toward the future. As we embark on this journey into the future, almost certainly we will see the newspaper as a manufacturing enterprise, the publisher of a printed product, shrink. But as a citizenry we cannot allow the newspaper as a news gathering organization to shrink.

The origin of this book was a graduate seminar on contemporary trends in journalism during the 2008 spring term at the University of Texas at Austin's School of Journalism. A small group of graduate students with professional experience in journalism who had returned to campus to study for their doctorates undertook the task of organizing the voluminous commentary and research on the future of news. Their task also caught the imagination of the faculty, 14 of whom prepared lectures and PowerPoint presentations for our seminar sessions. We express our deep appreciation for their work that set the foundation for this book:

- Dean Roderick Hart, *News consumers and the new media*
- Rosental Alves, *The impact of the digital revolution on journalism and journalism education*
- Paula Poindexter, *Will there be an audience for news in the future?*
- Wanda Cash, *How 'old' journalism fits into 'new' journalism*
- Dominic Lasorsa, *Exploring ways to attract tomorrow's news users*
- Mark Dewey, *Present trends predict the future*
- Tracy Dahlby, *Mediamorphosis in Asia*
- Iris Chyi, *Is online news an inferior good?*
- Amy Schmitz-Weiss, *Online journalism: Trends and challenges*
- George Sylvie, *Media management*
- Renita Coleman, *A brave new visual world*
- Homero Gil de Zuniga, *Role of alternative media in the democratic process*
- Robert Jensen, *News while/when the oil wells run dry*
- J.B. Colson, *Photojournalism in the contemporary era*

Building on these presentations, the chapters that follow set an agenda of perspectives to be carefully considered as we move into a new era of journalism.

Chapter 1

A Gutenberg Moment

David D. Brown

History has not been particularly kind to cultural fortunetellers, as tomorrowland visions of flying cars and rocket-propelled jetpacks vividly attest—but it has been notoriously unfriendly to those who have predicted the demise of various types of media over the years. Despite predictions, radio did not lead to the death of the newspaper, nor did television lead to the demise of radio or film. Each new development did, however, alter the trajectory of the technology that preceded it, lending credence to those who today argue that we are witnessing another mediamorphosis, the term coined by Roger Fidler to describe major transformations in the communication landscape resulting from the convergence of major social trends and technological innovations. According to this view, traditional forms of media will adapt—evolve—to embrace the promise of our digital age.

As of this writing, however, one can make a compelling—even alarming—case that what we face is not an evolution of communication but a *revolution* of such profound significance that it is impossible for old media to adapt; that the newspapers and broadcasts that used to provide our news will not survive this fundamental sea change in communication technology. What we are experiencing now is "not mediamorphosis, its media*cide*," says Rosental Alves, a journalism professor at the University of Texas at Austin. Scary stuff. Alves's implication is that news outlets that make themselves irrelevant are driving themselves out of existence. If news itself does not survive, what are the implications for the institutions journalism serves, such as community and democracy?

There is ample evidence to support both positions (i.e., "news is dying" vs. "no it isn't") and people are taking sides. If you are already a news professional or a veteran of a system of news influenced by large national media organizations and dominant players in newspapers and broadcasting, the future of news looks dismal, even threatening. The slow demise of big-city papers and loss of audience for nightly television news offers ammunition to those who see no future for traditional news. Ad revenues are down. Layoffs have become "business as usual" in newsrooms across the country. Jobs are being lost. Media empires are crumbling or merging to survive.

Conversely, people working in so-called new media (bloggers, citizen journalists, social networking aficionados and the like) see the digital era as liberating, promising freedom from the oligopoly of old-media. At the same time, many old-school journalists are learning to embrace new technology, using tools such as Twitter to promote and extend their traditional journalism online, break news and interact with the audience in novel ways. Young people are gravitating to the internet to get their news instantly, customizing content by selecting the subjects they want to read about with increasing ease and fluidity. Video-equipped cell phones coupled with the distributive power of the internet have made everyone a potential broadcast journalist. One example: after first accepting user-generated news stories and posting the best (most memorably, footage of the Virginia Tech shootings and the Minnesota bridge collapse), CNN has made its iReport a spot for unedited and unfiltered content, some of it of dubious quality and veracity. At other times, like the uprising in Iran after the June 2009 election, citizen journalism was the only available journalism.

But is this "news"? Moreover, is there a future for news if professionals are replaced by amateurs?

Perhaps a bit more reflection is in order. As futurist Paul Saffo warns, "Never mistake a clear view for a short distance." The truth about the future of news, as is almost always the case when talking about the "future" of anything, is likely somewhere in between extremes of current opinion. On the other hand, so much is in play in the world of digital media that pessimism about the future of news may be nothing more than fear … or, perhaps, a failure of imagination.

Admittedly, it could go either way. One of the most challenging aspects of thinking about the future, especially for those of us who spend time trying to isolate causes and effects in communication research, is fully appreciating and embracing the notion that change cannot occur in a vacuum. It goes without saying that the world is a complex system, but we sometimes need to be reminded that complex systems are not passive but adaptive. The observable changes we see today in the news industry may not represent ultimate effects of the digital era, but instead, intermediary effects in a transitional period of change. In order to make useful predictions about the future of news, we need to have a context—a lens—through which we can observe the changes we see around us. What seems to be happening so suddenly "now" in fact is more likely a series of causes and effects occurring over a much longer range of time.

OUR GUTENBERG "MOMENT"

On November 16, 2007, a columnist at the *Belfast Telegraph* became an international celebrity of sorts overnight. Less than 24 hours after the publication of his opinion piece, Kevin Myers' words were being cut-and-pasted and linked onto blogs worldwide:

> This is our Gutenberg moment, the watershed which divides one epoch from another, so much so that the inhabitant of the latter epoch cannot begin to understand what life was like in the earlier one.

Believe it or not, Myers was writing about the iPhone. No gizmo aficionado, Myers confessed he had very little idea of what the iPhone was, except that "it is, no doubt, the Swiss pen-knife of telephones."

> At which point, we turn a corner in civilization. If anyone anywhere can access the internet wherever they are on the planet, then the world is set to change in wholly

irrevocable and unforeseeable ways. In other words, the iPhone is probably going to have a greater impact on civilization than even television.

Perhaps. But for now, let's focus on Myers' larger, more general observation.

We're living in a Gutenberg Moment.

It's a phrase that rings with tremendous power, especially in the ears of journalists. The original Gutenberg moment wasn't really a "moment" at all, of course—nor was moveable type merely an invention. The "moment" was in fact a sweeping evolution in the way information—i.e., gathered, assimilated, edited, published, consumed and ultimately utilized. In Gutenberg's day, this moment represented a shift of information control from the political and religious elite to the commoner, the effects of which were unforeseen in Gutenberg's day. So, too, is digitization of ideas a transformative event with the power to eliminate information gatekeepers and alter flows of information, yet with much more rapid diffusion. Apple was selling more than 6 million iPhones per quarter by the end of 2009 and recorded the *one-billionth* downloaded application from its revolutionary App Store—all in barely two years. Once again, the keys to the control of information have been taken out of the hands of the relative few speaking uni-directionally to the masses, and the effects of these transformations are not at all plainly discernable. But history can be a useful guide, and what it points to is rather promising.

In the two centuries after Johannes Gutenberg developed moveable type, there was more intellectual advancement than in the thousand years preceding. Even at this accelerated pace of change it would be at least another two centuries before the emergence of what we might recognize as "news" in a traditional sense with standards and practices and a quasi-professional class of news practitioners. The digital age, by comparison, is still quite young; by this measure alone, sweeping pronouncements about the death of journalism seem quite premature.

To avoid confusion, let's not get hung-up (so to speak) on the iPhone. It is just an early convergence device. Like the first internet browser, the iPhone may be obsolete in a few years. What matters is that communication convergence is feasible, not fantasy. Once-impersonal activities such as watching television can have the intimate aspects of one-to-one interpersonal communication.

So despite Myers' colorful prose, the introduction of a single consumer device like the iPhone is probably not a transformative moment per se. But functionally, what the iPhone represents can be a useful metaphor to help us gain insight on a larger shift in the realm of communication—one with clear implications for the future of journalism.

THE "FILTER" SHIFT AND END OF MASS MEDIA

Our Gutenberg moment might be said to have started at any of several places in the age of electronic media, but it may be useful to imagine the dawn of the digital era at the end of World War II with the invention of the transistor at Bell Labs, the ongoing refinement of the binary computer, and the development of the U.S. Defense Department's ARPANET system for long-distance computer-to-computer communication (the precursor to the internet).

Each of these developments, and the many that have followed, facilitated a convergence of what futurist Roger Fidler has defined as the three domains of communication as we humans have known it: interpersonal communication, communication via document, and electronic communication. Although each of these domains can be said to have distinctive characteristics, the latter two domains—that is, the innovations of communication via document and electronic communication—serve as proxies for interpersonal communication over distances of time and space. In other words, letters, notes, television broadcasts, radio transmissions, record transcriptions and so forth are functionally bridges that allow us to share ideas by "leapfrogging" problems of speakers and receivers being separated by physical or temporal distances.

The iPhone (or something like it) illustrates the likelihood of nothing less than the ultimate *convergence* of the three domains of communication—*the closing of a circle.*

If, in the palm of one's hand, one can communicate interpersonally (via text, audio or video), access and contribute to databases containing virtually every written document ever stored (via the internet), and transmit and receive images and sound (once the exclusive province of licensed broadcasters), then all the rules have changed: all communication effectively takes on attributes of interpersonal communication. One can transmit pictures and audio to someone whenever, wherever they are—and that person, in turn can react and respond by transmitting pictures and audio irrespective of time and distance.

Historically, information technologies have been used as portals to selectively redistribute knowledge and provide access to information from entities of control (such as governments, media organizations) to the masses in a uni-directional flow. This model allows easy commoditization of information. If these information technologies are now available to all, the resulting effect is to make communication not merely bi-directional, but omni-directional. One by-product of this change is to shift the importance of the information "filtering" process from the transmitter (editor or other information gatekeeper) to the receiver. In theory, at the very least, this change would logically mark the end of "mass media." Overstatement or not, this "filter shift" has profound implications for the future of publishing.

Already the digital era has sunken titanic fortunes and created new ones. The music industry, for one, has been shaken upside down by its ankles. Analog formats (records and tapes) have been replaced by a parade of digital alternatives (compact discs, mini-disks, digital audio tape, mp3s and wavs, to name just a few). Recording studios have been rendered obsolete by laptop computers. Jobs have been lost—from engineers and executives to publicists. Empires have crumbled. But it's vital to note what endures—individuals' desire for music. From 8-gigabyte portable music players to music-playing phones to the videogame rage that is "Guitar Hero," popular music is still the rock star it has always been.

In this light, the resilience of traditional news outlets in the digital age is rather amazing: a testament, perhaps, to the particular skills involved and benefits a still-sizable segment of society perceives it has derived from news delivered via television, radio and newspaper. Still, the arrows all seem to point in one direction. Down.

A recent report on the future of news by the Carnegie Corporation of New York lamented, "broadcast television's evening news programs, for example, are no longer the family hearth that brings people throughout the country together at meal time." Television news networks no longer deploy dozens of high-profile correspondents around the world; indeed, CBS News (once the crown jewel of the "Tiffany Network") reportedly talked with CNN in 2008 to repurpose (re-use) cable news reports, and network and local broadcasters were involved in content-sharing marketing agreements from Miami to Los Angeles. Likewise, afternoon newspapers have virtually disappeared in most cities, leaving just one morning edition surviving. Although the *New York Times, USA Today* and the *Wall Street Journal* are available on street corners throughout the country, the daily audiences of national news websites dwarf the circulation of the big three.

But note: None of this, per se, implies that the news product as we've traditionally known it is no longer desirable or useful. That inference has to be drawn from a separate line of evidence showing a gradual, apparently generational decline in "news interest" (or to be more accurate, interest in traditional media forms such as newspapers and television network news broadcasts) coinciding with the rise of digital media—but apparently not sparked by it. Researchers have measured declines in "news interest" since the 1950s which will be further addressed in chapter 2.

Prior to the rise of popular web use, declines in "news interest" were usually linked to a decrease in civic participation—a line of reasoning that tended to finger "mindless" television as the chief culprit. This line of argument culminated in Robert Putnam's famous essay and book *Bowling Alone*, which in part blamed the lack of civic involvement on the increased time Americans spent watching television. It is not unreasonable to suggest that blaming digital media for declining "news interest" may be merely swapping scapegoats.

Likewise, we must be careful not to confuse declines in newspaper readership and television news consumption with the demise of news.

Indeed, the persistence of news interest among internet users is an obvious sign of an ongoing demand for news in the digital era. News consumption has become continual, although the nature of "news" is increasingly defined by users instead of traditional gatekeepers. In an era of easy access to raw information on demand, the traditional job of the reporter—to assemble facts, draw inferences and generate a narrative—is increasingly the domain of end users. The act of searching or Googling for new information about specific or timely events has become "a new paradigm," according to the 2008 report on American journalism by the Project for Excellence in Journalism.

On this rudimentary level, at least, wondering if there is a future for news is akin to wondering if there is a future for curiosity. In this sense, the question is almost circular. *Of course there is a future for news.* It just may not be *your* news or your idea of news. Although the digital era surely means transformations in the content and character of "news" in the future, for end users, the question is rhetorical and somewhat absurd.

The reason this answer doesn't satisfy most of us, in large part, is that we're not really asking if there's a future for news. *What we are really asking is, "Will I still have my job as a reporter/editor/publisher/journalism teacher in 5 or 10 years?"*

One of the most damning indictments of traditional media comes not from the blogosphere, but from practicing journalists themselves. If anyone should be free from the sin of hubris, it should be the journalist, seasoned in objective assessment. And yet a "journo-myopia"—a unique form of hubris—flourishes at this hour as the influence and power of mass communication fades into the history books.

Mass media is not a prerequisite for news any more than sidewalks are a prerequisite for walking; the former merely facilitates the latter.

The death of mass media is not the death of news.

GETTING BEYOND "JOURNO-MYOPIA"

For a $20 admission fee, visitors can tour one of the most expensive museums ever built in Washington, D.C., a seven-story edifice called the "Newseum." It took four years and almost half a billion dollars to build the steel-and-glass structure devoted entirely to the history of mainstream media. It is tough for tourists to ignore the free admission signs at other nearby museums all over town.

"(The Newseum's) success is premised on the false belief that the public is as impressed by mainstream media as mainstream journalists are, reflecting a similar disconnect between news outlets and their consumers," Washington University journalism professor Steve Boriss wrote on his blog The Future of News. "It is often said that pride comes before the fall. Perhaps that should be etched into the side of the building as a fitting epitaph to a dying industry."

From Boriss's perspective, blogs like his own represent the "Davids" to the corporate media "Goliaths." Clearly, blogs are a phenomenon of the new media age, but the connection to diminished interest in news is circumstantial; while more people are reading blogs (and linking their own blogs to other people's blogs), mainstream media has been unable to find a way to monetize the phenomenon of this interactive media. The American Press Institute concluded that "(t)he hype of blogs, podcasting, user-generated content, video newscasts and email news alerts has swept many newspapers onto the bleeding edge, when in fact, few of these features generate any ad dollars."

On the other hand, there is plenty of evidence to show that younger people are more likely to read blogs than to read a daily newspaper. According to the Pew Internet and American Life Project, by 2006 the internet had become the primary news source for people under age 35, and a 2008 Pew report found the number of people who get most of their political news online had tripled since 2004. Of those who use broadband four or more times a day (so-called "power users"), more than 70 percent go online for news. Moreover, the study says that younger readers, often dismissed as uninterested in news, "are being drawn into the news habit earlier" because of the internet's appeal as a source.

As a source for news, however, the internet is a virtual buffet. Blogs, YouTube posts, discussion boards and trend monitors all supplement websites from traditional news sources like BBC.com, CNN.com, NYTimes.com, or from new "digital establishment" players such as Google News, AOL News or Topix.com. More significantly, the news consumer of the digital age is "brand promiscuous," dividing their news use time among 12 to 16 brands per week across virtually all media platforms (radio, TV, newspapers, magazines and the internet), according to research by the business consultancy McKinsey & Company.

"Just because print circulations are declining does not mean there are fewer news consumers. In fact just the opposite is true," according to Jack Flannigan of comScore, a firm that measures internet usage habits. "Non-newspaper readers are, in fact, heavier than average news consumers."

In a March 2008 report, comScore found that younger generations growing up getting news for free will probably signal the demise of newspapers—but not news. "The internet represents a significant opportunity to extend—even improve upon—existing news brands and reach out to new consumers with living, breathing real-time content." In fact, comScore found that among the 21 million Twitter users in late 2009, the fastest growing cohorts were users 12 to 17 and 18 to 24.

The trends also confirm what many have suspected about the changing habits of news consumption—that people have adapted to the age of information proliferation by becoming "news scanners," consuming bits and pieces of information from a variety of traditional and non-traditional sources, digging deeper on certain subjects of interest, and assembling their own private narratives in order to "connect the dots," that is, in order to understand their world.

This process of synthesizing the truth is a familiar one to most traditional reporters, who daily triangulate sources and contextualize facts when trying to tell a cohesive story. Carl Bernstein, one half of the team that cracked the Watergate affair at the *Washington Post* in the early 1970s, has long claimed that journalists offer the "best obtainable version of the truth." But it is increasingly probable that "better" (i.e., more personally tailored and therefore more relevant) versions of the truth will abound as information consumers form their own information constellations, assembling the facts as they see them … right or wrong, for better or for worse.

Veterans of traditional journalism will quickly counter that this isn't really "news" at all: that the activity of gathering facts and assembling them is empty without regard to core values, that is, without editorial distance, without verification of allegations or other facts, without a sophisticated understanding of source motivations—all of the values that have distinguished American journalism for most of the 20th century. Indeed, critics are correct to point out that maintaining these core values is central to the preservation of traditional journalism. Nonetheless, they increasingly exist in a professional vacuum, less appreciated than ever before by the people they purport to serve. In the digital world, traditional journalism is not perceived as a service, but rather as another "voice."

In the McKinsey study, respondents did not generally differentiate between blogs, online editions of traditional newspapers or online opinion journals (such as Salon or the Huffington Post). They explained that the reasons they consumed so much information about current events from such a wide variety of sources (traditional and non-traditional) was that "there are two sides to every story," or "to get all the facts," or "to form my own opinion."

Efforts to migrate newspapers to the web have, for the most part, failed because new journalism is not merely old journalism repackaged for distribution on the web. Such a perspective fails to take into account that it is not just technology that's changing: it's the way people consume information—how we incorporate information into our daily routines, and how we process, aggregate and internalize the growing landscape of information we are exposed to. We are becoming part of a larger information environment that transcends (or at least incorporates) traditional journalism.

This is at the crux of it: "New media" are not merely a new form of media (another technology for journalism to adapt to), rather, "new media" describes the way people are shaping technology to suit their information needs and habits. And we are only at the beginning of a long journey.

This does not mean that traditional journalism has become worthless, or that there is no future for business based on journalism in the media landscape of the future. But if traditional media outlets continue to answer the challenges of the digital age by pursuing media strategies that cut core newsgathering resources, then their most valuable assets—their reputations—will wither. If, for example, the *New York Times* loses its reputation for quality international reporting, it simply will not survive. On the other hand, even if the economies of print force the *Times* to abandon newspaper publication, it is nonetheless possible for the *Times* not to merely survive, but to thrive in the future.

There is an important role for traditional media providers if they are willing to (1) become service oriented—that is, help digital-era consumers (news scanners) meet their needs on their own terms; (2) think in entrepreneurial ways about business models for journalism-based enterprises (rather than as newspapers or news broadcasts), and; (3) cultivate their brands as assets, north-stars in an expanding galaxy of information.

THE NEW NEWS BUSINESS IN A POST MASS-MEDIA WORLD

The Media Center at the American Press Institute published a media briefing entitled "Synapse" a couple of years ago. It was a four-page burst of trends that could be gleaned from (then) current developments in information exchange online. According to the report, citizen journalists, independent news reporters, online guides, and street videographers will disintermediate access to news and information leading to a future for news that is:

- Global in scope
- Accessible everywhere, anytime
- Transparent
- Participatory (a conversation, not a lecture)
- Edited for more, not less
- Funded through a variety of services and access points
- Reliant on social entrepreneurship
- Authentic
- Dependent upon simple trust

Some of these values may be idealized and somewhat naïve. For example, there's no reason to preclude an interest in local issues, nor is there any reason to think that the public at large will not, over time, become jaded by the "fake authenticity" of corporate voices pretending to be independent. Likewise, it is easy to confuse the end of mass media's "one-way street" with its romanticized opposite, the "conversation." Conversations assume at least two sides with mutual respect for each other's opinions—otherwise, they fast become diatribes and ultimately monologues; countless online communities have sprouted up and gone extinct for this very reason.

Instead of focusing on the traits of *users-as-new-media-publishers*, a more durable and realistic set of observations should isolate the fundamental shifts both in *users-as-consumers* and in the technology that makes the new media environment what it is—mobile, specialized, immediate, entrepreneurial, visual and participatory. Through this lens (and probably vastly better ones still to be articulated), it is possible to identify attributes of an information or news-based business for the digital age:

- Niche/Speciality content (to capitalize on fragmentation)
- Deeply Linked and Interconnected (permitting more digging, more "click-throughs")
- Multi-platform (to take advantage of "scanning" habits; creating additional revenue streams of repurposed content)
- Noisy and Brand-focused (to distinguish the voice and stand out from other voices on the web)
- Investigative (or otherwise exclusive) Information

Attempts by traditional newsrooms to capitalize on the digital transformation have been, up to now, more a function of scrambling to backstop the tremendous losses in print and broadcasting. As of this writing, journalists who manage to survive layoffs at newspapers are being asked to be scribes, photographers, bloggers, reporters, and otherwise jacks-and-jills-of-all-things-internet. Some newspapers have tried to harness the public's interest in self-publishing by creating virtual communities online and posting blogs and videos edited to a greater or lesser extent. Both are likely to be passing fads because neither strategy has shown any sign of being economically self-sufficient. This represents old media fumbling in the dark for direction.

But even though the rules of the media business have changed, the rules of business *innovation* have not: winners provide a service that is faster, better, *and* cheaper than the competition in a given environment. Given that necessity is the mother of invention, it is of no surprise that new experimental models are, literally, making news. Harvard's *Nieman Reports* shared five new nonprofit models whose support comes from philanthropic readers, foundations and corporate sponsors. Long-standing media institutions like the Carnegie and Knight foundations fund experimental journalism among entrepreneurs, news outlets, and even college journalism schools, which turn the classroom into a newsroom. Once news businesses get a fix on the competition (nonprofits, news aggregators, individual blogs, user-generated media sites and the like) it becomes quite possible to imagine at least four possible paradigms for new media news operations.

1) The freelance hyperspecialist

The new journalist will not necessarily be a Swiss army knife, but an entrepreneur building an information business out of a core expertise unrelated to journalism, per se. For example, one might imagine Dan Neil, Pulitzer-Prize winning automotive writer for the *Los Angeles Times,* striking out on his own with a website that becomes the locus for a variety of automotive-related news, reviews, sneak previews, advice, audio journals, and the like built around his identity as a likeable, witty, celebrity expert. The basic revenue generator would be the "click-through" model, which earns advertising money based on the number of page-views, but at this scale of operation, it is foreseeable that a successful hyper-specialist could employ a modest two- to three-person staff to help generate content, and operate and promote the business. The product is expertise—offering something that can be considered "the best there is" in a given information specialty. Journalists (or news organizations) will become so expert in their knowledge about a given subject, they will be valued as oracles.

2) New publishing houses

The New Publishing House will be a company with pre-existing resources to both: (1) sustain audience-building over a five- or 10-year low-profit timeline, and (2) ultimately generate massive amounts of *open* content across many specialties—not mass media, but "multitude media." As news audiences become more highly specialized, with sites for nearly every political interest, vocation, avocation, geographic and cultural focus, new publishing houses will exploit this fragmentation and sell highly targeted audiences to advertisers trying to maximize impact. This strategy is already working for Time Warner's America Online (a former digital age innovator all but left for dead, according to conventional wisdom). AOL is fast becoming a new media giant, publishing a range of highly specialized and highly successful websites including TMZ (celebrity journalism), AOL Money and Finance (business news), Switched (technology), Asylum (male-oriented), BlackVoices (hip-hop culture) and URLesque (web trends). The scale of the enterprise as a whole makes smaller profits at any one website sustainable for long-term cultivation and development.

3) Boutique (or "intelligence") companies

These approaches operate on a model somewhat inverse from the New Publishing House. A news boutique generates one channel of extraordinarily high-quality *closed* content, available at a premium to subscribers. Digests such as *The Week* and *The Economist* are templates of this new format—and, not coincidentally, both niche publications enjoying growing print circulations. *Hoovers, Quorum Report, Texas Weekly,* and Stratfor.com are all early success stories based on this model. And major mass circulation media have moved back and forth in recent years on the question of open online access for all content versus fees for some or even all content. The *Wall Street Journal* online is entirely subscriber-based, and its success as a "superior good" led publisher Rupert Murdoch to announce plans to charge access fees across his line of News Corp. publications online. And a number of local daily newspapers have now closed all or most of their content. The continuing question is where the revenue will come from to support quality journalism.

4) Content management services

This is an individual or company or website providing a service in a manner not unlike that of a money manager overseeing financial portfolios. For persons or corporations with a vested interest in filtering good "intelligence" from bad (that is, taking advantage of information that may be of high value but low trustworthiness), a content manager becomes the end user's "information filter" for a fee—performing the function of a human news aggregator with editorial judgment and operating on a set of specific instructions. Each content management service contracts with news content providers, scans the web constantly for potentially useful information, and may operate its own news content provider as a boutique.

It is far easier to declare the death of news than to imagine its survival, much less actually put at stake one's own fortune in search of the new horizon. But for traditional media companies, the choice is quite simple: continue to cut back and hope that the attrition will stop before the money runs out, or restructure and reinvest existing resources in innovative new media enterprises. Only the latter strategy can yield a successful outcome, and even in the worst-case scenario, new media "failures" will be no more bankrupt than those who chose to ride out the storm.

NEW NEWS, OLD QUESTIONS

The historic premise of how a free press and the skills of journalism bind together democratic institutions merits a certain reassessment and reality check in light of the changing nature of news in the digital age. The mass civic audience is fragmenting, and mass media are disappearing. News consumers evince increased skepticism about the credibility of the so-called mainstream media, viewing the internet as a "work-around." Meanwhile, some social critics express concern about a growth in cynicism about civic affairs and a concurrent rise in the importance of money and single-interest groups. Is there a connection between the fall of old media and civic fragmentation? Can democracies function effectively without the cohesion provided by traditional media? Some worry that there are major issues we all need to be plugged into as a common community: issues such as global warming, education, a healthy democracy, an economy that gives people jobs, and healthcare. As audiences become more fragmented, the puzzle for news becomes how to get common civic information to mini-audiences. Failure to do so, some argue, would be a failure of American journalism to live up to its end of a grand democratic bargain—one that secured the development of a robust, constitutionally protected free press tradition that has set the bar for the rest of the world.

Perhaps we see the emergence of a kind of "celebrity" democracy (since celebrity journalism seems to be becoming the only genuinely shared mass media experience to be had in the near future), which elevates shallow, inexperienced but glamorous politicians and red-carpet causes above others. But this is wholly speculative because the democratic process itself is not likely to remain stagnant, and this co-adaptation of media and democracy is likely to make it very difficult, indeed, to determine whether new media is having a salubrious effect or a deleterious one.

These are still early days. Ten, twenty years from now, it is entirely possible (indeed, probable) that we will see a new set of interests emerge as communities redefine themselves, as multi-polar communication becomes more ubiquitous, and as the real world, itself, faces a new array of challenges and new generations of interests. It is not at all inconceivable that some cataclysmic event might generate (one might say re-generate) a new public affairs interest that more closely resembles the mid-20th century mass media heyday, albeit in a different (digital) forum.

If that happens, the difference will almost certainly be that the common, shared super-agendas of the future will be largely driven by consumers, not by the information gatekeepers of the past who have set our agendas for decades. Tomorrow's public affairs agendas will probably correlate with the five or six topics most people are actively seeking information on at any given time, in other words, the five or six public affairs issues most actively monitored or scanned by the greatest number of information consumers.

Our "Gutenberg moment," if it means anything, is that the published word as we've known it will no longer be the province of those who own the presses and the transmitter towers. Just as the "gatekeeper" function of the priests and political elites evaporated in an earlier communication revolution, our "Gutenberg moment" promises to make it possible for anyone with an idea, no matter how small or insignificant to reach as many as are willing to pay attention. In the grander sweep of history, this is nothing more than the further democratization of information. The evolution of news is an inevitable byproduct.

Yet critics will continue to wring their hands, warning that this turn inevitably leads to a dilution of valuable or important information—a kind of information overload. Plato warned of a social vertigo of ubiquitous opinion, banning opinionated artists from his Republic. Perhaps too much information is a genuine danger. However, thus far in human history, information overload has been a hypothetical problem more than an actual one. One can imagine this very argument of information overload being used during "Gutenberg I:" "What *are* we going to do with all those books that will be published?"

Then as now, we need not fear too many voices.

SUGGESTED READING

Fidler, Roger (1997). *MediaMorphosis: Understanding New Media.* Thousand Oaks, CA: Pine Forge Press.

Jenkins, Henry (2006). *Convergence Culture: Where Old and New Media Collide.* New York: NYU Press.

Shirky, Clay (2008). *Here Comes Everybody: The Power of Organizing Without Organizations.* New York: Penguin Press.

Chapter 2

Dark Days Ahead

Kelly Kaufhold

"Honestly, I don't follow the news that much," says Gerald Goodridge, a 21-year-old college student. "If I'm sitting there waiting for class I'll hit up CNN.com on the cell phone. I'll watch the election coverage a little bit, but other than that I don't really care." Goodridge is a pretty typical 20-something news consumer—which is to say, he isn't one. He doesn't read a daily newspaper or watch television news and when he does go online, it is mainly in search of sports information or for social networking. By the way, Goodridge isn't just a college student. He's a journalism student, one of three dozen interviewed about their news consumption habits.

The sardonic question in journalism schools is, if there are no future consumers for news, then where do students plan to work? Each year the humor yields a bit more to the reality. In an age of historic circulation declines, newspaper employee buyouts, dwindling television ratings, any "future of news" is going to look indescribably different from the ghosts of journalism past. Chapter 1 argues that news will look different, be found in different places, but that it will always "be." If the chapter you just read is *A Midsummer Night's Dream*, this one is *Macbeth*.

Skeptics of the pessimistic view say not to worry; when the young aren't young anymore they will follow the news. The conventional wisdom goes like this: young people don't read newspapers because they aren't fully invested as citizens. When they have a spouse, children and a mortgage they'll have much more need for news, just as their parents did. CBS News president Andrew Heyward shared this optimism on *NewsHour with Jim Lehrer* in 2002:

> Time is on our side in that, as you get older, you tend to get more interested in the world around you … . So I think you become more engaged with society as you get older.

In fact, a 2008 *Newspaper Research Journal* study found that even slightly "older" young adults followed the news more than their youngest counterparts. Half of those aged 25 to 29 said they were interested in news compared to only a third of 18 to 20-year olds. And there is substantial data showing that Americans over 50 are a lot more likely to follow the news than those under 30.

But those numbers are misleading. The overwhelming majority of older Americans who read a daily newspaper or watch a daily newscast have had the same media habits since they were 20-somethings, even teenagers. Most of those over 50 who don't read the paper now, never did. David Mindich's book, *Tuned Out: Why Americans Under 40 Don't Follow the News*, shows that those who don't consume news in their teens and 20s aren't likely to pick up the habit as they age—a fact borne out through studies of the parents of today's under-40s. Their parents started "tuning out" in the 1970s and each subsequent generation reads and watches less news than the generation before. People who were non-viewers in the 1970s are largely non-viewers to this day. And the losses in newspaper readership are even more precipitous.

Forty years ago, eight out of ten Americans read a newspaper every day and many read more than one. In fact, just after World War II the average U.S. household received 1.3 newspapers a day, on average—a morning edition with that first cup of coffee, plus an afternoon paper on the doorstep after work and after school. Yes, even young adults and teenagers read the paper. In 1965, two-thirds of Americans under age 35 read a newspaper every day and more than half of them watched television news. By 1990 only one-third read a newspaper and barely two out of five watched television news. Clearly, Gerald Goodridge isn't the only young adult not following the news.

American newspaper circulation is now falling at 7 percent a year, on average. The *New York Times*, the nation's second-largest daily newspaper, lost $74 million in a single quarter in 2009 and is circulating at 1976 levels. Mexican telephone company billionaire Carlos Slim loaned the Grey Lady a quarter of a billion dollars—to cover payments on the *Times'* other $1.1 billion in debt. McClatchy Co. reported a $100 million drop in revenue on the back of $2 billion in debt from the purchase of Knight Ridder. Paying the piper is becoming ruinously expensive.

"So?," you say. "It's the newspaper. Nobody reads the newspaper anymore, but people still follow the news—just look at the increase in online traffic." In fact, research presented to the Midwest Association for Public Opinion Research found that young adults followed news and engaged in politics. Americans under 30 were more likely than older Americans to go online for news, to read and write on blogs, and to interact on social network sites. Goodridge, the journalism student, is online a lot—in fact, he was online during the interview for this chapter, checking on the NBA playoffs on ESPN.com, watching highlights on YouTube and checking his Facebook page. He and many of his friends are online, but they often aren't pursuing news. Young adults participate differently—but they still participate less than those from older generations. They read less news, know less about current events and are still less likely to vote, even in the digital age.

About half of online users do follow news, but as with traditional forms, like print and broadcast, online news consumers tend to be over 40, and they also tend to be the same people who have long bought a paper or watched a newscast. Newspapers and television stations have migrated content to the internet; first original content, now unique fare offered only online, often in hopes of luring new people to their audience. News outlets earn their keep from advertisers, not readers or viewers—a barter system, of sorts. Traditionally, readers would agree to pay a small price for a paper to be counted in readership numbers; television viewers would make an appointment to watch TV at the time the commercials ran. Now, news outlets offer the same content, but time-shifted and at no cost—the same news any time, anywhere, and for free. Business analysts have words for this, like substitute goods and information surplus. I call it cannibalization.

Online revenue is growing in the newspaper industry, and in dramatic fashion—up 35 percent in a year. But because of cannibalization, that isn't enough to compensate for precipitous declines in print circulation. The Audit Bureau of Circulations, newspapers' official arbiter of doom, confirms that U.S. newspapers are losing 3.5 percent of their circulation every six months. And even while audiences for online news are growing steadily, they're not enough to bridge the gap of lost advertising revenue. Research shows that it takes anywhere from 20 to 50 online readers to make up, in terms of ad revenue, the loss of a single print subscriber. Publishers from top U.S. newspapers met in May 2009 to look for a reprieve from the failed economics of giving away content. Among those proposals for how to put the genie back in the bottle—a micropayment plan from Google, the largest distributor of free content.

In that *Newspaper Research Journal* study from 2008, young adults said they intend to spend more time following the news and less time on social networking and watching video clips in the coming years. In fact, they expect to triple how much time they spend with daily newspapers while cutting their online social networking by more than half. On this evidence alone journalists would be ill-advised to spend money they don't have buying champagne, because unless this is new math the numbers don't add up. This would be the first generation of young adults to actually act on these intentions. All signs suggest that traditional news consumption—not only print and broadcast, but online consumption of traditional news outlets—will continue to fall.

In 1964, more than a third of Americans read two newspapers every day. Nearly nine out of ten read at least one newspaper—86 percent. Now? Forty percent. Television viewing is still migrating from the broadcast networks to satellite and cable channels, but again, all viewers are not equal and the problem isn't confined to the United States. The *Financial Times* in 2004 noted that in Belgium over five years, news viewership fell 6 percent overall—but 15 percent among 16 to 34-year olds. A 2006 study in the *Journal of Broadcasting and Electronic Media* quantifies the current state of affairs in the United Kingdom. Nearly half of high school seniors were either involuntary (21 percent) or intentional (28 percent) news avoiders.

Young adults still turn on the TV, but for entertainment, not news. Young men, especially, may not be watching broadcast, cable or satellite, but rather playing a video game. If young adults in, say, 2000 acted on their intention to follow more mainstream news in the future, the contemporary audience would be growing—not shrinking. Researchers describe young people like these as "news avoiders." Young adults, those under age 35, are half as likely as those over 40 to watch news on TV, whether it's Katie Couric, Wolf Blitzer, or Shepard Smith. This isn't lost on the journalists whose livelihood depends on television news viewers. A 2008 survey by the Pew Center for People and the Press put it this way:

> Speculation over Katie Couric's future as anchor of the CBS Evening News has raised the broader question of how long the three nightly network news broadcasts will be able to survive.

Forty-two percent of national journalists expect the three network nightly newscasts to have permanently faded to black within a decade.

So the thesis of this chapter is that young adults don't read the newspaper, don't watch TV news, and when they are online it largely isn't for news. Overall, readership of newspapers is falling at the fastest year-to-year pace on record and even the most reliably stable publications are joining the fall. The *Los Angeles Times* has cut its staff in half in 10 years. "Mediasaurs" call it a vicious circle—fewer journalists produce an inferior product, and the *Los Angeles Times* has cut the size of the paper by a dozen pages. But the decline in revenue preceded job cuts by decades. Television newscasts that once garnered ratings of 30 are now drawing single digits.

"Ah," you say, "but about one-and-a-half million people still get the *New York Times* on any given Sunday." True, and two million see a *USA Today* or *Wall Street Journal* during the week; and on any given weekday evening, perhaps 20 million Americans will keep their appointment with the nightly network news. America's informed democracy isn't dead, but it is running a fever.

University of Texas journalism professor Rusty Todd puts it bluntly: "The newspaper will die when its readers die." But newspapers aren't news, as was so ably argued in Chapter 1. The contemporary landscape features two competing philosophies: a *Daily Me*, personalized for individuals, versus a role for "gatekeeping"—for news professionals selecting and editing what "we" need to know. Bill Kovach and Tom Rosenstiel, in *The Elements of Journalism: What newspeople should know and the public should expect*, describe it this way:

> The primary purpose of journalism is to provide citizens with the information they need to be free and self-governing.

And Thomas Jefferson wrote:

> Were it left to me to decide whether we should have a government without newspapers or newspapers without government, I would not hesitate a moment to choose the latter.

In other words, journalism is important. It helps people decide how to vote, where to spend their money, which way to drive to work. The argument is that better-informed citizens lead to more accountable leaders. The problem isn't dwindling newspaper readership, or less attention to television news. Critics wary of cohesion between the media and government are missing the point. Journalism, as intended by the founding fathers, is at the service of citizens as the source for information about governance. Of the importance of a free press, Alexander Hamilton wrote, in *The Federalist* number 84:

> What are the sources of information which the people ... must regulate the conduct of their representatives in the ... legislature? Of personal observation they can have no benefit ... They must therefore depend on the information of intelligent men, in whom they confide.

Aside from the obvious target painted by the phrase "intelligent men" in the press, the problem is this: An uninformed public undermines democratic society. David Mindich, in *Tuned Out: Why Americans Under 40 Don't Follow the News*, used age to examine both news consumption and political interest. As one might expect, the two correlate strongly. Those of retirement age have nearly triple the interest in politics as those aged 18-24. News interest more than doubles from the youngest to the oldest cohort. The disparity widens even more with regard to certain media franchises. For example, those aged 45 and above are four times more likely to listen to National Public Radio than those aged 18-24. In fact, the youngest adults barely listen to NPR more than teenagers. Those 20- and 30-somethings are much more likely to follow popular culture, like *American Idol*, than anything political. Remember that comScore report on Twitter in chapter 1? So what are those young people sharing on Twitter? Hollywood celebrity news. Young people are online, they're embracing internet information sites and they're sharing with each other. They just aren't doing any of this with real news.

The danger—and it is naïve to think of it as less dire than that—is that the coming lack of news consumption by a generation of Americans will correspond with a lack of political knowledge, interest and involvement. The very governance of America will be yielded to those who can manipulate the small percentage of citizens necessary to sway the vote.

NEWS BRANDS

Information "brands" if you will—NPR versus *American Idol*—represent a generational divide over what is news. Critics (especially critics over age 40) question the credibility of some new media sources, like blogs, or entertainment outlets like E!Online or MTV. One school of thought says established media "brands" like the *New York Times* or CBS News carry a well-earned credibility that comes from decades of professional reporting; the other says established outlets rely too much on reputation, bordering on arrogance, and that they're just too slow. "After a while, you have to change with the times," says Joseph Millares, a 20-year old journalism student. As for his local newspaper, "It's not quick enough for me. I get all my news from my phone now, or from my laptop."

Think about news aggregators, like Google or Yahoo News, MSNBC.com, the Drudge Report, or about hybrid aggregator/blogs like the Huffington Post or MichelleMalkin.com. Those sites offer links to handpicked stories from a variety of news outlets, some traditional mainstream, some not. "Gatekeepers" at legacy media like the *Washington Post* carefully report and write stories, weigh their importance, select how to frame them and design the layout of the page. This routine plays out in each of America's 1,430 newspapers and in all of the newsrooms operating in the 210 distinct television markets. Prominence, headlines, and images all are analyzed and sorted according to established rules and traditions which include, among other things, at least a genuine attempt at thoroughness, objectivity and fairness.

But once online, this news content becomes a sort of information free agent, available at no cost for redistribution with no rules. Aggregators or hybrid sites can change a headline, change the framing, and place a link to a *Washington Post* article between links to *The Daily Show* and PrisonPlanet.com. And the blogs then contribute to the content, allowing instant and ideological responses to articles—responses that often eventually exceed the length of the article itself. In the case of prominent sites like the Huffington Post or MichelleMalkin.com, the popular blogs become destination content themselves. Does this dilute the original brand name? Or does the association with a traditional brand increase the credibility of the aggregator? Do readers even check the brand name in a link? Finally, who decides on the credibility of a brand?

Media veterans confidently believe that the decades-long traditions of some outlets ensure their rightful place as the arbiters of news. "The newspaper of record," as it were, or "Murrow's boys" at CBS. Yet, a legitimate contemporary criticism is that both the *New York Times* and CBS News have stumbled badly in recent years. Each institution was perhaps deceived innocently enough by rogue employees or shabby reporting, but each ran erroneous content nonetheless. *U.S. News and World Report* editor-at-large David Gergen served four presidents and now directs the Center for Public Leadership at Harvard's Kennedy School of Government. He describes media credibility with unmistakably potent language, calling it "the coin of the realm."

But ... what if the story of interest is Jon and Kate's marital woes or *Dancing With the Stars*? Four million Americans aged 18 to 24 voted in the 1998 midterm election but 24 million Americans, most of them under 30, voted in the first *American Idol* finale in 2003. Thirty-seven million Americans watched the second presidential debate between Al Gore and George W. Bush in 2000; 40 million watched *American Idol*. This illustrates another pitfall for mainstream media. Since *Enertainment Tonight* first aired in 1981 and *USA Today* hit newsstands in 1982, local newspapers and television news outlets have migrated more toward mimicking these formats, adding more color, more features, and more entertainment news. Perhaps that was sensible policy in the dark ages of analog media. But think about the concept of credible sources and marry that with an interest in, say, news about Brad Pitt and Angelina Jolie—then consider the most credible source. So while local television news outlets may cover celebrity scandals and movie releases, experienced fans know they can learn more at the *Hollywood Reporter*, TMZ. com or the Internet Movie Database. Newspapers increasingly offer feature video online, like a slam-dunk in a local basketball game, but YouTube can cue up those clips by the dozens. These are the stories that go viral on Facebook and Twitter.

So, the question is, do brand names matter? "For the journalist, maybe," says Goodridge, the 21-year old journalism student from the beginning of this chapter. "But I don't think it's important to the public as far as the ideology of it. I mean it's only going to matter if you get it wrong." This illustrates another potential pitfall in contemporary "news." For many years, some listeners have had trouble distinguishing between talk radio and news, despite the protestations of radio hosts like Rush Limbaugh that they were entertainers, not journalists. Online, people newly exposed to endless information may well have similar trouble distinguishing between "real news" and opinion, or information and entertainment. So how does someone like Goodridge determine whether information is right? "That's where Google comes in."

INFORMATION SEEKING

News sources, the places one can go for information, fall into three broad categories:

1. **Impersonal Traditional**: A smorgasbord of a handful of gatekeeper-selected items, which includes what has been called "eat your peas" journalism, like your local newspaper. This has long been the model of traditional news, with the only available alternatives in the pre-digital dark ages being specialized publications or outlets that offered more depth, like the *New York Times*, news magazines or public radio. This is news for people who not only don't object to major media setting their news agenda but who depend on it. Now, one can select agenda-setters of a particular stripe, which dilutes the traditional media functions of agenda setting in the first place—and may undermine the value of objectivity.

2. **Personal Directed**: The directed part implies a deep bore through multiple sources into a single issue. Examples of personal directed stories include an impending hurricane, a close election—even information about promising athletes on NFL draft day. This type of news consumption previously existed in specialized fashion, as well, in publications like *Fantasy Football* or through marine weather radio reports. The difference between pre- and post-digital is that one had to take active steps, at some expense, to "join the club" and access the information. Now, in some fashion, all information is available to everyone, any time online, usually for free.

3. **Personal Undirected**: This implies information on a multitude of topics from multiple sources, automatically aggregated and custom delivered (via e-mail, or RSS, or wireless device). Much of this information gets ignored although it was probably, at some point, selected by the user who signed up to receive news from certain sources via specified pathways. This also applies to those who may glance at headlines on a social networking news stream or browse the home page on YouTube. It isn't really about news at all, but rather, about information—usually entertainment.

To make a case that this is problematic requires a bit of journalistic arrogance. Is there real value to media elites setting the agenda for citizens? Is this issue salience between the agenda builders (politicians, policy makers), the agenda setters (journalists) and the audience important? Or is it just a quaint reflection of the 19th and 20th centuries? After all, the modern mass-media model began in 1835, with the first non-partisan, objective penny papers reaching millions of Americans a generation before the Civil War. David Brown ably argues in Chapter 1 that traditional mainstream media can be arrogant, as evidenced by the half-billion dollar Newseum. But is it arrogance or accuracy? Reputation or reliability? There is a case to be made that professional gatekeeping is a good thing, that it is "eat your peas" journalism. In fact, the argument that the *New York Times* maintains a reputation on the skills of its international reporting cadre is quite right. Perhaps news is a bit like coffee; there used to be one kind that could be served in a couple of different ways. Now there is a dizzying array of choices on the information menu.

The criticism is that issue salience between governing elites and media elites is just "information insider trading," a game played by the well-connected in Washington and New York. The defense is that reporters and editors don't arbitrarily select their stories—they weigh them through a variety of established gatekeeping parameters, including importance and relevance to citizens. There is a reasonable tradition of covering the stories that are important—stories that objectively and realistically matter. That importance risks being lost in an era of self-selected news.

SOCIAL NETWORKING

Perhaps the greatest irony of all in a world of six billion people is that the future of news might be one-of-a-kind. It's the *Daily Me*, an aggregated, customized version of information—not necessarily news—put together on the spot for an individual client. Anyone familiar with Facebook or MySpace knows how malleable those online tools are, with hundreds of shareware applications and tens of thousands of groups, any of which can be downloaded, joined, mixed and matched. Facebook launched in 2004 and now has 100 million active users—those who have logged in within the last month. Overall, there are more than 200 million members. Stephen Colbert, of Comedy Central faux news fame, has more than 1 million friends on his account. The Pew Research Center for the People and the Press found that two out of three young adults online (those under 30) used social networking sites. (By the way, Facebook employs only 500 people; MySpace, only 300.)

Facebook and MySpace both offer news applications, and users can also personalize information on Yahoo and Google, and even on mainstream outlets like MSNBC.com. Services like Spotback not only let users customize content but "read" user traffic and customize it themselves. In the spring of 2008, Royal Caribbean announced an online social network to let former cruise passengers stay connected with their shipmates and employees with whom they developed relationships while on board. Clearly there is a vibrant and diverse future in online social networking, and news will play a role.

To be sure, for people who spend hours online each day, social networking, watching and sharing videos, keeping up with entertainment, there are opportunities for news to be found. Many of the must-see sites online, like Facebook, Google, AOL and MSN, feature news headlines on the home page. This is the electronic version of gatekeeping, since there is some selectivity—a "page 1A" mentality—to the headlines that run, and because most of these stories link to mainstream news outlets, like wire services or major newspapers. "I think that's what I focus mainly on," said 21-year old student Tracee Brewton. "It's easy when you're just on Google and you see them. You click on a headline because it will spark your interest." And when a group of students was asked if they will click on an interesting headline the answer came in unison: "Yeah." But when asked if they'll delve for more information about an interesting story or seek out multiple sources based on a single deadline, they again answered in one voice: "Not really."

The internet has revolutionized social networking. Robert Putnam, a public policy professor at Harvard University, studies social capital—the threads between individual neighbors that get woven into the fabric of community. He has argued that television viewing, which became widespread in the 1960s, tore at the seams of social capital by taking people out of the communities and parking them inside, alone in front of a glowing screen. But people parked in front of glowing screens aren't alone anymore.

Internet-only communities come in two broad forms: those that link people from far-flung corners of the world, united by a common interest, and those that serve as an electronic social calendar for friends and neighbors next door. Social networking sites like MySpace and Facebook serve both roles, creating a clearing house for people around the world seeking, say, car parts for 1960s Sunbeam Alpine sports cars, but also coordinating Thursday night happy hours in downtown Seattle. In fact, Facebook originated at Harvard exclusively for students at that institution and then spread through the Ivy League and to other college campuses. It is still largely organized around college and university groups, which require the appropriate ".edu" e-mail address for admission to certain groups.

Like e-mail, the advantage offered by social networking sites is the ability to disseminate a message to a wide network of people in about the same time it would take to notify one person. But the architecture of these sites is much more consuming than that. Social networking accounts allow for hundreds of photos, categorized and labeled; quick-reference lists of current and potential friends; public and private ways to communicate, including open threads for running conversations, in public, with multiple users; electronic "graffiti walls" for messaging; virtual gifts, drinks, and much more. Music downloads, once a proprietary commodity, are now a staple of social networking sites.

OPINION LEADERS

So everything, from choosing a bar to planning a party to inviting friends to posting pictures afterward, is handled from one source—a source now available via mobile phones. The sites even identify and alert users to potential new friends, those with common acquaintances and interests. Online networking of this type is a sort of virtual vortex for all things social, including what Elihu Katz and Paul Lazarsfeld called "personal influence." Their seminal post-WWII book, *Personal Influence: The Part Played by People in the Flow of Mass Communication*, elucidated the role of opinion leaders in presidential elections but the idea is woven throughout social fabric. Everyone knows a social butterfly, a party organizer, a take-charge boss, or the best-dressed mom. Those are opinion leaders. In a pre-electronic age, people walked to the corner store or beauty shop for the news and gossip that made them a part of the community. It was an oral tradition that governed interpersonal communication for millennia, but now that's often done online. Communication, even mass communication, is interpersonal but unlike traditional mass media, such as a television newscast, daily newspaper, or CNN.com, messages can exist in a user-generated bubble, insulated from reaching people outside the network.

So what are the implications for news? "The news will find me," says blogger Paul Kedrosky, who has drifted away from news blogs because of what he calls "info-clutter. I had largely stopped going, mostly because I didn't have time and wasn't finding enough interesting stuff."

I interviewed 36 college students throughout 2008 and 2009, asking them about their media habits. Even among the journalism students, the results weren't reassuring for traditional, mainstream journalists. Of the 36, only three were regular news consumers and only one could be described as a habitual newspaper reader—albeit always online. Two commonalities emerged among all the students about their current media use, which was not restricted to traditional news. First, all compulsively text on their phones—it's the primary method of communication. Second, online social networking, like Facebook, MySpace and Twitter, are primary sources of what these students need to know. And what they need to know is information about their friends, their clubs and their classes. Their most common and trusted source for information was a friend, via e-mail, social networking or a phone. Their most common exposure to mainstream news was by accident. "If I'm home and I'm flipping channels and I come across a newscast I'll sit there and watch it," said Tracee Brewton, a journalism senior. "Or if I'm on the internet I'll go to a news website and read it. It's easy when you're just on Google and you see them. You click on a headline because it will spark your interest." Most others only watched TV news when it was already on in the dormitory cafeteria—never at home. Other news sources cited by these students included Yahoo!, Facebook and YouTube. "I'll just search random videos," said Femi Salami, an accounting senior, who often starts on YouTube. "You know how they'll have recommendations? Then I'll just kind of click through these."

The reason this matters is because it's human nature to choose the entertaining over the depressing, the familiar over the new. There are people who will choose the peas over the pizza, but there aren't many of them—especially among young adults. Metaphorically, this is the situation created by the revolution of web technology. "News" does find its way to these young people, but it isn't what, say, the editor at the *Washington Post* intended to serve on their plate. "My friends send me different news information that they think would be interesting," said a senior studying nutrition, who gave this example of interesting news: "They discovered the real-life Furby. It's uh, it's an animal in, like, Indonesia they thought it was extinct but it's not … it looks like a Furby" (which is a children's toy).

An Associated Press-commissioned study of young adults called the problem "news fatigue," describing a bewildered population of Americans aged 18 to 34 drowning in a cornucopia of news, unwilling to sort the important from the trivial. The study describes young people as having "trouble accessing in-depth stories" and being "inundated by facts." The AP confidently redesigned news delivery to adapt to the shorter attention span of these news avoiders. They needn't have bothered. As in the 2008 *Newspaper Research Journal* study, young adults will sheepishly admit to a need to follow the news, even promise to do so more in the future or if the news better fit their needs. Then they'll ignore it unless it's titillating enough to turn their heads for a minute or two. The problem isn't information overload so much as information selection. Candy sells pretty well online—veggies, not so much.

That's the risk posed by social networking and the opinion leader process. If someone with hundreds of friends finds something interesting to pass along, off it goes, and if a viral video becomes popular online, the link can reach more than 1 million inboxes. But Kedrosky defines what is valuable to many members of these online communities—"interesting." For those already interested in news, personalization is a revelation. For others, it just offers more tools with which to avoid the news. Opinion leaders determine what gets passed on through the network—will it be the latest quarterly economic indicators, rising tension between Israel and Iran, three history-making presidential candidates? Or the latest celebrity break-up?

The viral networks do sometimes infect users with news—for example, Barack Obama's Democratic response to President Bush's 2008 State of the Union Address was viewed more than 1.3 million times in the weeks after the speech. What's missing from this calculus is part of our definition of news: the professional journalist. Facebook users aren't interested in objectivity or balance and YouTube doesn't have an equal time rule. Presidential candidate Obama had more than one million social network "friends," which tripled the tally of his Democratic rival, Hillary Clinton, and was eight times the number for Republican John McCain. A *New York Times* article referred to it as "replacing the professional filter—the *Washington Post*, clicking on CNN.com—with a social one."

News isn't always about sexy, or funny, or enthralling. Sometimes it is all those things—who could turn away from their television on Sept. 11, 2001? But sometimes it's mundane—how commissioners are spending tax dollars or which roads will close for construction. Those "eat your peas" stories—local, hard news stories—are at greatest risk if traditional journalism dies. Absent local, professional journalists, one might ask who will cover local government, taxation and spending, and scandals? Citizen journalists who maintain blogs deliver what has been referred to as authentic journalism. But when money is on the line and the future is at stake, which information is more important—authentic or accurate?

The optimists make a compelling argument that a cataclysmic event could re-infuse young Americans with a "need for news" and there's evidence to that effect from the 9/11 attacks. But as with all things news, there is a generational caveat. The Sept. 11, 2001 terrorist attacks led to a sharp spike in news consumption, but even in the shadow of this cataclysm, Americans aged 50 and above were twice as likely as those under 30 to closely follow the news and those young adults who did "tune in" for a bit were much quicker to tune out again than their older neighbors. This wasn't a study of newspaper reading, it was a study of news consumption. If the defining tragedy of a generation isn't enough to awaken an interest in news among youth, what is?

THE FUTURE IS BRIGHT—FOR THOSE WILLING TO PAY

What some academics envision as the future of news online is a growing cadre of high quality, specialized niche sources for information, something already taking shape. Those working in finance and in the media have long been familiar with subscriptions services like Bloomberg and the *Wall Street Journal*, the only major American newspaper still able to command an online subscription fee. The *Economist* and Stratfor.com offer competing financial news. The advocate says this niche or boutique news is good—it provides a reliable source for important information, slicing through the clutter of the internet's Wild West, delivering the right information at the right time to those who are willing to pay, benefiting those who need it and can afford to pay for it. Some scholars describe a future with hundreds of new premium sources, micro and even hyper localization and audience targeting, and an increasing skepticism and irrelevance surrounding traditional media. The economics of digital information mean information delivered with high precision at low cost—the opposite of mass media. But what of the great unwashed who are seeking the same information online? The increase in brand-name niche offerings promises to widen the gulf between the haves and have-nots. Success may breed success leading to subscription sites for other types of content … like news. The other side of the coin is that Yahoo and Google both offer channels with free access to a wealth of company information, financial news and share price histories to guide investors.

A GLIMMER OF HOPE

Let's revisit how these concepts apply to young adults back in the real world. College student Joseph Millares is 20 and doesn't mince words about whether he follows the news. "No. I stopped reading newspapers after [a reporting class] because I didn't need to anymore." Mindich, in *Tuned Out*, surveyed more than 100 Americans under age 40 about general political knowledge and found only a handful who could, for example, name their U.S. senators, several Supreme Court justices, or the three countries then-President Bush called "the Axis of Evil." But among those few who did follow the news, Mindich found some important similarities. For one thing, they had some external influence that increased the importance of staying current—a boss who was well informed, perhaps, or a business owner whose clients closely followed current events. The need for news was a vital and sufficient cause.

They follow the news for the basest of reasons—because they have to, a calculus sometimes lost in today's family, educational and media environments. Since the maturation of the Baby Boom generation, an expanding portion of Americans just haven't felt a need for news, which has contributed to dwindling percentages of people with reliable media habits—not only traditional mainstream media, but even new media news avoidance. Media outlets have tried to modify their content, altered their designs and styles, customized the offerings for members of certain demographics and now personalized the content and delivery of information. These techniques all focus on the information providers, the communication sources. There is a radical school of thought that asks a different question altogether, one that isn't popular because of the view it takes of the customers.

What if the media isn't broken—and the audience is? What if many millions of Americans, because they were never expected or required to, just don't have a need for news? Mindich, in *Tuned Out*, introduces students from Bishop Perry school in New Orleans who understand the need for news. They are expected to be well prepared for guest speakers and they're also involved in international civics projects, so they regularly read both local and national newspapers. Many of those students report being *New York Times* subscribers years later, as high school students. The most remarkable part is that Bishop Perry is a middle school and the subscribers are 12 years old.

"If news were food I wouldn't be this skinny," says 26-year old Caleb Pritchard, a history buff and recent graduate with a bachelor's degree in journalism. "I check the *New York Times* website compulsively, every five minutes all day. I wake up every day and spend probably two hours in bed going through the *New York Times*, *Austin American-Statesman*, CNN, CNN Politics,

Al-Jazeera, BBC, ABC." Pritchard's fingers haven't been darkened by newsprint in years—he gets all his news online. But when he goes web surfing he's looking at mainstream news sources. "I have all of those in my bookmarks. I try to cycle through those every day."

Pritchard believes that he consumes news much more than his peers and he clearly remembers when he started paying attention to the news 15 years earlier. "Ever since elementary school my friends and I would always be the political nerds and the snobby we-know-everything kind of guys. If you didn't know something you were shunned. If I don't know something I feel like I can't really participate in the conversation. It feels kind of weird." And it doesn't happen often.

A FUTURE FOR NEWS?

So is there a future for news? Established "brands" will remain, perhaps targeting a segment of the audience for whom there is enough interest for the news producers to exact a subscription price. Certain blogs will succeed because they offer enough unique reporting to attract a regular and loyal audience. And given the revolutions of both the internet and wireless devices, "information" will be ubiquitous. Personalization will ensure that certain people receive certain information in more detail and greater quantity than ever before and those with diverse viewpoints will be more empowered and validated than at any time in history. But news avoiders will be empowered as well.

John McCain often talks about the five years he spent as a prisoner of war in Vietnam. He suffered isolation, torture, hunger. But, he says, "The thing I missed most was information—free, uncensored, undistorted, abundant information." Prichard spent two years at a military school, from 1998 to 2000, and describes a similar deficit. "We had maybe 30 minutes of NPR in the morning, the small daily newspaper, *USA Today*. It was terrible because I wasn't able to follow the war in Bosnia. The Clinton impeachment I know nothing about." He views journalism as the first reading of history.

Fortunately for journalists, he also offers a future.

SUGGESTED READING

Mindich, David T.Z. (2005). *Tuned Out: Why Americans Under 40 Don't Follow the News.* New York, Oxford: Oxford University Press.

Kovach, Bill & Rosenstiel, Tom (2001). *The Elements of Journalism: What newspeople should know and the public should expect.* New York: Crown Publishers.

Neil, Henry (2007). *American Carnival: Journalism under Siege in an Age of New Media.* Berkeley, CA: University of California Press.

Poindexter, Paula, Schmitz Weiss, Amy & Meraz, Sharon (2008). *Women, Men and News.* New York: Routledge.

Chapter 3

Attracting Tomorrow's News Users Today

Dominic Lasorsa

THE NEWS OF the future is being shaped by important trends of today. Dramatic shifts in the media landscape are confronting journalism with unprecedented challenges. Major social, economic, and professional trends raise critical questions about the news industry of tomorrow. By addressing the implications of these trends in imaginative and visionary ways, however, these challenges can be turned into opportunities, opportunities to create a more stable, more appealing, and more healthy media environment. Taking the lead on moving the news business into the future could be a relatively underutilized resource: the journalism school. The future of news depends upon how well the journalism profession is able to reconceptualize the news of the future.

Four major well-documented and well-known trends affect the production and reception of news today: (1) news proliferation, (2) news audience fragmentation, (3) news migration online, and (4) news owner concentration. These four strong currents are related and move together to influence a fifth major trend, one of enormous social consequence: media trust deterioration.

NEWS PROLIFERATION

Recent technological innovations are changing both how news is gathered and produced and how news is accessed and processed. Bloggers, citizen journalists, tech-savvy freelancers and other new types of communicators have the potential to affect the very nature of news and how it is disseminated. Simultaneously, internet portals, instant messaging, handheld devices and other new means of communication have the potential to affect the very nature of audiences and how they are reached.

News arrives from an astounding assortment of sources. In the United States, there are about 1,400 daily newspapers, 6,800 weekly newspapers, 1,600 broadcast television stations, 8,500 cable systems, 13,000 radio stations, and 28 million blogs. Adjusted for population, the situation is similar in many industrialized democracies, especially in Asia and Scandinavia. For example, the United States prints 212 daily newspapers per 1,000 persons, South Korea prints 343 and Sweden prints 446.

One effect of such an overabundance of media choices is that people can feel inundated. Freedom of choice is almost universally revered and underlies all notions of democracy. However, too many options can overwhelm us. Unless we have sufficient contextual information to allow us to evaluate alternatives, a multitude of choices becomes debilitating, not liberating.

Today's highly competitive news business environment also has encouraged the idea that news is whatever sells and, as the news media have made efforts to attract younger audiences, hard news has lose ground to soft news. As a result, more news today is being offered without much context. Morsels of news presented with little background or perspective can make the reception of news by audiences more baffling than illuminating. The multiplication of choices consequently makes it harder to find *quality* news amid the *quantity* of news. The result is too much "news" with too little news value. The overall effect of this is that people may come to devalue the news and, in turn, those who gather and report it.

NEWS AUDIENCE FRAGMENTATION

In addition to the bewildering amount of news, it is being increasingly segmented into distribution systems targeted to different social groups. In New York City, there are 274 ethnic newspapers and magazines published in 42 languages, including 27 daily newspapers. In Chicago, there are 250 ethnic publications, and across the United States there are thousands of culture-focused periodicals and broadcast stations. These media cater to audiences who want news about their communities and the places from which they came, news they do not receive from traditional news channels. These cubbyhole publications are taking advantage of the "long tail" phenomenon. While a few large news media outlets like the *New York Times* reach huge audiences, there exist many more smaller news media outlets that still have a niche audience from which they can profit.

The long tail business model has generally been regarded as a challenge to the big, well-established players, and an opportunity for their upstart rivals. Major bookstores, movie rental outlets and music chains, for example, can carry only a fraction of available books, movies and music. The traditional outlets therefore focus on the top sellers. However, the point of long-tail commerce is that audiences have a much wider scope of interests and, given the opportunity, will purchase the lesser-known products that inhabit the long tail. So, while Borders bookstores display about 100,000 books, Amazon.com displays 3.7 million. It is estimated that e-commerce businesses makes 20 to 40 percent of their profits from long-tail sales.

The long tail, however, offers opportunities for traditional businesses, as well. Newspapers have been slow to take advantage of the new communication technologies. Their online forays have often resulted in an internet presence that is not much different from their paper product. Seeing the online world as mostly a threat rather than an opportunity, they have failed to take advantage of the possibilities for growth that lie in the long tail. The daily newspaper has always envisioned itself as a mass medium, giving the same set of stories to everyone. However, most news stories are read by only one in four readers. In that sense, the mass media have always catered to a segmented public. The internet simply gives the media greater opportunities to serve those sub-publics with wider and deeper coverage. Newspapers could vastly increase the news they offer online and give their readers the tools to find the types of news they want. However, if newspapers do adopt the long-tail model as a means to better serve their readers then we should expect an even greater segmentation of the news audience, that is, even more sub-publics.

Media that satisfy myriad tastes will undoubtedly appeal to the individual consumer but the impact on society as a whole may not be entirely positive. What is the effect of progressive segmentation of the news, of sub-publics essentially living in their own small worlds, increasingly isolated from the worlds of others?

When news is customized for different social groups, its meaning may change. Facts and sources may be included or omitted, depending on the nature of the target audience. Not long ago, national television newscasts reached most citizens, exposing them to a common rendition of the news of the day. By focusing on local issues and events, local daily newspapers and local newscasts encouraged a sense of community. A newspaper can be defined as a community having a conversation with itself. In today's more highly fragmented news environment, one might ask, "How do you keep the world from becoming hyperlocal?" While news always has been framed to suit audiences, the increasing departmentalization of news may also encourage people to perceive that news as relative. If news seems increasingly tailored to fit the expectations of particular segments of the population then questions about its veracity grow and audiences may begin to discount it. This, too, can lead to an erosion of trust in the news.

NEWS MIGRATION ONLINE

There is little doubt that more people are getting more news online and that young people especially find online news appealing. Certainly, people are making increasingly greater use of the internet. Young people, in particular, are heavy online users. However, general internet use does not equate to internet *news* use. Access and time-spent data are far less valuable than observations of the specific activities in which internet users actually engage. Entertainment contributes little to political knowledge and participation; learning about politics and public affairs is much more likely to come from *news* media use than from mere media use.

The internet is second only to local television news as the primary source of news among young adults (118-34 years old). Although this age group is the most likely to be online, they also are the least likely to follow news online. Among men, high-income groups, and high-speed internet users, the top two ranks are reversed. As broadband access increases, making internet use even more pleasant for the consumer, we can expect internet news use to accelerate.

Traditionally, use of news increases with age. As people move from childhood to adulthood, they become more interested in community affairs and their attention to news consequently grows. Use of newspapers, national television news, local television news, and radio news all increase with age. One potential problem is that the issue isn't only which medium one uses (the oldest Americans prefer newspapers; Baby Boomers, television; Generation X, the internet). Just what people choose to follow on TV and online (entertainment versus hard news) also plays a role. While more young Americans spend more time online, research by journalism scholar Dhavan Shah and others has shown that Baby Boomers are more likely to follow *news* online.

The greater use of internet news by younger people reflects the *general* appeal of the internet to them, coupled with the lesser appeal of other sources of news. When asked whether they thought they would be using various major news media more, less or the same in three years, 44 percent of young adults in a 2006 survey said they intended to be using the internet more for news. In contrast, considerably fewer said they expected to increase their use of any non-internet news sources. A 2007 survey of college students did find that they intended to follow mainstream media more—but so far, they haven't acted on those intentions.

Beyond mere exposure to the news media, the *depth* of exposure can be ascertained by asking respondents the extent to which they used a medium to *seek* news. The depth of news exposure increases from teenagers, to young adults, to older adults. Even though teens use the internet for news more than do young adults, who use the internet for news more than do older adults, it is still the case that seeking out the news on the internet, as well as from the traditional news media, increases with age. This counters the argument that people are abandoning the news. Instead, people, most especially younger ones, are abandoning traditional sources of news in favor of online sources of news. People have not so much lost interest in news—that would seem counter to a long-observed human tendency and what may even be a basic human instinct. What may appear to be a general decline in news interest may in reality be a major audience realignment as audiences gravitate to online news sources.

Furthermore, young adults are no different than their older counterparts when it comes to what they want from news sources. The two most important factors when selecting a news source are trustworthiness and being up to date. The internet outperforms all other news media on being up to date but compares significantly less well on trustworthiness. The internet also is evaluated poorly against the newspaper on having few advertisements but outperforms it on every other feature, including alerting people to damaging or harmful situations, offering news they can use, being a useful way to learn, being entertaining, and providing news only when they want it.

The appeal and convenience of the internet as a news source, coupled with the feeling that the internet is a less trustworthy news source, may create a sense of cognitive dissonance among users. Feeling conflicted about using a source of news they believe may be less credible might make consumers devalue further the news and those who produce it.

Of interest also is a trend that troubles some journalists and educators. Younger news consumers appear to be moving toward a preference for news with opinion, or at least an admission of opinion. The 18-34-year-olds resist the notion of an objective journalism more strongly than do older adults and they also say that news presenters should be transparent in their assumptions, biases and history. This may help explain the popularity of news personalities such as Rush Limbaugh and Keith Olbermann whose programs unabashedly present the news with ideologically based and emotionally laden commentaries. Younger people appear to have less respect for traditional journalism than do older adults, and this may lead to a further erosion of trust in news media generally.

OWNERSHIP CONCENTRATION

Despite the proliferation of media outlets, many are being gobbled up by a small number of huge conglomerates. A half-dozen multinational corporation—Bertelsmann, Disney, General Electric, News Corporation, Time Warner, and Viacom—now control the major U.S. media. What is the effect of such media consolidation of ownership? The notion that just a few major corporations disseminate much of the news which citizens receive troubles some of us. News consumers fear that these conglomerates may have other priorities beyond solid news production. In addition, this suggests to some that the idea of myriad choice of news products may be more of an illusion than real, with the same few voices simply repackaging the same stories for different audience segments. Furthermore, these companies now compete in a cut-throat economic environment in which the bottom line is the bottom line.

While the tension between revenue and quality has always existed in the news business, the concentration of ownership has exacerbated the pressure to profit. In the tug-of-war between news quality and corporate revenue, some fear the news is losing. Such suspicions can lead to further distrust of the news industry.

DISTRUST OF THE NEWS

It appears, therefore, that each of these four major news industry trends is contributing distinctly to a fifth major news industry trend: growing distrust of the news profession and those engaged in it.

Relative to other professions, public trust in the news media has not been strong. For decades, the Gallup Organization annually has tracked more than 25 professions, including medical doctors, college teachers, clergy, bankers, business executives, advertising practitioners and lawyers. Journalists receive a middling performance rating, consistently appearing in the middle of the pack. Furthermore, while individual professional ratings do not tend to change much over time, the rating of journalists' honesty fell from 33 percent in 1977 to a low of 21 percent in 2000. (The rating showed a significant hike the next year.) Police officers also got a big boost in their rating in 2001, and firefighters, who were ranked for the first time in 2001, got the highest ranking of all professions. The rankings of all three professions, however, retreated in 2002. These three professions, which during the September 11, 2001 terrorist attacks were highly visible—often dramatically engaged near ground zero—may have benefited from that salience when the survey was taken a few weeks after the 9/11 attacks. The public's trust in these three professions seems to have been affected by their performances during that tumultuous time. Since then, however, these professions' ratings have dropped.)

Other polls have shown a similar downward trend in trust in journalism. For example, the Pew Research Center for the People and the Press reported that those saying they can believe most of what they read in their daily newspaper declined from 84 percent in 1985 to 54 percent in 2004. The results were similar for both broadcast and cable television news. In 1985, 55 percent of Americans told the Pew center that news organizations get the facts straight. Since the mid-1990s, however, the majority of Americans have said that news organizations do not get the facts straight. In 2007, 53 percent of Americans said news stories are often inaccurate.

The believability ratings for individual news organizations are consistently lower today than they were just 10 years ago. A 2009 Pew study placed news media trust at its lowest level in nearly 30 years of polling on the topic.

Being skeptical of the news media, however, is not an entirely negative sentiment. Audiences hold images of the news media as institutions that have consequences for both how they use the media and how much they learn from news media content. Those who believe that there is an underlying pattern to the news learn more from news content. Also, having some doubts about news quality helps rather than harms learning by stimulating more careful attention.

In other words, a bit of healthy skepticism is a good thing. Nevertheless, the deterioration of trust is an enduring trend that has implications both for the future of the journalism and for the future of political systems worldwide.

The erosion of trust in the news is directly related to the other news industry trends mentioned here. The overall result of these four other movements—news explosion, audience segmentation, online emigration, and owner consolidation—is a cacophonous amalgamation of news sources of all stripes, from international correspondents to infotainers, from TV anchors to radio shock jocks, from cable pundits to political bloggers, from podcasters to paparazzi. Together, these changes in the media landscape can give the impression that news is subjective, relativistic and commonplace. The overall effect is a cheapening of the value of the news and a lessening of trust in those engaged in its production.

IMPLICATIONS FOR DEMOCRACY

While most nations claim to adhere to the essential principles of democracy, significant deviations exist. For example, the Constitution of the Democratic People's Republic of Korea describes that nation as a democratic state, but others find little evidence of democracy in North Korea. Basic democratic principles include majority rule, protection of political minorities, respect for basic human rights, equality before the law, and due process. Government based on the consent of the governed is the defining feature of democracy. Democracy therefore presumes the existence of free and fair elections. The news media are implicated in the democratic process because they are expected to provide the intelligence necessary for a citizen to make an informed political decision.

Some argue for the need for "strong democracy," which goes beyond the basic conception of merely providing free elections. Strong democracy emphasizes the efforts of average citizens to control their lives and the performance of media in promoting informed participation by citizens. The idea that a free, independent press is essential for the existence and maintenance of democracy has been widely endorsed among modern democracies. The question becomes, "As the media landscape changes, will the news media be capable of sustaining that informed participation?"

Since education levels in most modern democracies have been growing steadily, one would expect a corresponding increase in citizen engagement. Instead, it has diminished. In the United States, political knowledge, voting turnout and other indicators of a healthy democracy have remained stagnant or have declined in recent decades. The only exception is youth volunteerism, which has increased primarily because youths now are being compelled to do volunteer work as part of their school work.

The trends in news proliferation, news audience fragmentation, online news emigration, traditional news exodus, news media consolidation, and news media distrust affect the ability of the news media to strengthen citizen engagement and to promote a strong democracy. Given the burgeoning number of news sources available, audiences need help separating the wheat from the chaff. One way to help audiences identify quality products is to establish clear standards to judge quality. The ever-increasing numbers of nontraditional news organizations and bloggers, some of which are trying to shape public opinion and policy, should be considered journalistically on their own terms. The journalism profession should set standards for them that apply to what they do and the ways they do it.

Standards that reliably indicate excellence usually have been identified through a process of licensing. Professions generally license practitioners who are then held to those standards. In most modern democracies, however, a movement toward licensing of journalists has not occurred. At a 2006 meeting in New York about the future of journalism, not one of the more than 40 industry and university leaders present said they favored the establishment of a licensing system. It is clear that licensing of journalists is not a popular idea and is not going to happen any time soon. Where, then, can we look for help in setting professional standards? One place where we might find such guidance is the journalism school.

Indeed, there are steps journalism schools could take to reinvigorate journalism around the globe, to seek consensus on the fundamental ethical issues confronting the profession (e.g., the appropriate use of news sources), and to speak with a voice of authority that clarifies the standards of journalism and the importance of quality journalism in a democracy. Journalism schools at major research institutions could do what they do best, to collect crucial data and to experiment with new ideas. Journalism schools have the tools to experiment with different models, to analyze what works and what doesn't work.

Journalism schools could collect definitive information on how news habits are changing. They could help news professionals understand better what audiences want. Journalism schools could collect definitive information on how news is used in all levels of schools to teach civics, history, writing and other subjects, and they could explore ways to use news more productively in classroom settings. If young people can be taught the importance of news at an early age then they are more likely to carry that into adulthood.

Journalism schools could experiment with new media forms, helping editors and publishers re-envision their organizations as more than simply distributors of their own creative products but instead as participatory community institutions in which they embrace ideas and input from outside their own walls. Journalism schools could help traditional news media see the internet as more than a mere supplement to their existing operation but instead as an essential ingredient in new product development.

Journalism schools could fashion symbiotic relationships with news producers to create innovative news programs that break new grounds of coverage. PBS's excellent investigative series *Frontline* recently formed one such successful relationship with the Graduate School of Journalism at the University of California at Berkeley.

Journalism schools could play a seedbed role to develop novel ways to cover news across the globe. International reporting has become increasingly and sometimes prohibitively expensive for the networks to cover with full teams of correspondents, producers and camera crews. The schools could help pioneer ways to use new technology, such as empowering students to use handheld cameras, cell phones and other devices to gather and report the news. Beyond concentrating on the traditional media, journalism schools could embrace more fully the new media and learn how to produce quality journalism better and cheaper, what *Frontline* executive producer David Fanning calls "garage start-up journalism."

Journalism schools could even consider underwriting quality news media in their communities. There is no reason why foundations and other nonprofit organizations cannot purchase or run news outlets devoted to quality news. A news organization intending only to break even can emphasize coverage it believes society needs. Nonprofits could pay more attention to those being less served by news media that increasingly target affluent consumers. Successful nonprofit models already exist, including the Associated Press, the *Christian Science Monitor*, the Public Broadcasting System, and C-SPAN. Even some daily newspapers are nonprofit, including the *St. Petersburg Times*. Overseas, nonprofit journalism has a long history. For example, the British Broadcasting Corporation and the *Guardian* are both nonprofit news operations.

The news industry and journalism schools have a long and unfortunate tradition of speaking passed each other. In these times of rapid changes in the media landscape, all of which seem to be negatively affecting the people's trust in the news media, the time has finally come when the news industry is looking desperately for help to solve the serious problems plaguing it. News professions have never been more willing to listen to journalism schools. It is time for journalism schools to speak up and to help make news in the future more appealing to those who need it most.

SUGGESTED READING

Connell, Christopher (2006). *Journalism's Crisis of Confidence: A Challenge for the Next Generation*. New York: Carnegie Corporation of New York.

Goldstein, Tom (2007). *Journalism and Truth: Strange Bedfellows.* Northwestern University Press.

Hamilton, James T. (2003). *All the News That's Fit to Sell: How the Market Transforms Information into News*, Princeton University Press.

Chapter 4

The New Newsroom: Changing Job Roles and News Organizations

Amber Willard Hinsley and Amy Schmitz Weiss

Rachael Myrow began working in the news industry at the dawn of the internet era for journalists. Information could be verified with a few well-directed point-and-clicks, relevant news could be gleaned from a quick perusal of others' websites, and PR lackeys could be sidestepped with to-the-point-emails to sources. "All this made me much faster at my job than editors and reporters functioning solely off of physical papers and handwritten rolodexes," she says, adding that other leaps in technology aided her speediness. In her field—news radio—time is a defining characteristic. Producing quality reports is as important as producing them quickly, and new devices that allowed digital recording helped in that endeavor. "I could mark a new track at the moment I heard something I knew would make a good cut. I once produced a four-minute feature in two hours," she says.

If Myrow represents the typical journalists' use of the internet and new technology, then Mike Linder was a journalist living on the cutting edge with his use of the web. Early on, he embraced the internet's capabilities and combined it with advances in technology that led to some of the first war reporting supplied solely over the internet. He created "Berserkistan" in 1995, with his teams of young reporters fanned out over Bosnia, conducting interviews and taking photographs of the atrocities there. "They embedded themselves in military units before the term was coined," he says. The teams would drive to Croatia to file their stories and photos through an AOL dial-up service and Linder, stationed in Los Angeles, would edit and post the materials. The site averaged about 50,000 hits per day, a monster number in 1995. "We were read by the White House, War Crimes Tribunal, countless NGOs and Bosnian refugees worldwide, and linked to on the brand-new CNN website," Linder explains.

Myrow and Linder's experiences illustrate the everyday and advanced ways journalists have adjusted and adapted the ways they go about doing their jobs and raise the question of what the newsroom of tomorrow will look like and how journalists will in fact "be journalists." Consider the following scenario, in which the hypothetical "Samantha" represents how many journalists do their jobs today and how many more will transition to this new role:

Samantha is heading downtown to cover a rally, a bag slung over her shoulder with a laptop, mobile device, some multimedia equipment, a small notebook, and a pen. As she walks to the subway to catch her train to get downtown, she is downloading details about the rally to her mobile device. She has already identified specific individuals and com-

munity leaders who will be at the rally through the use of some contextual locators, which serve as an online library of information, on her mobile.

As she boards the train, she has a map on her device showing where the rally will be held and how she can use this map with her story. As the train departs the station, she writes a question into the mobile management system that connects directly to the news website and she asks the public what they think of the rally. She also skims some social networking sites, looking for what people are saying about the planned rally, and posts her question on her profile page, encouraging her "followers" to provide feedback there or on the news website.

During her seven-minute ride, Samantha is already thinking of the individuals she will interview when she gets to the rally, including what photos, video and audio she will capture, and may use her social networking sites to connect with others at the event to get some of these materials. As the train pulls into the station, her contextual locator downloads a series of articles from previous rallies that have been held in the city and she will use these for context in her story. She checks back to the posts she made asking the public their thoughts on the rally and finds dozens of responses already. She knows she will need to go through those responses fairly soon so she can incorporate some of them into her story.

As she walks to the rally, the crowd is building and she can hear shouts in the distance. Her mobile device clicks and she instantly connects to her colleague via video, telling her not to forget to get the exact coordinates of the rally location so they can place it in the digital map when she posts her first piece on the rally. As Samantha enters the event, she begins to smile and her enthusiasm builds knowing that she is in the heart of her story and is ready to fully jump into the news reporting stage.

Samantha represents the future of journalism and she has the ability to embrace a new work environment that is digital, versatile, mobile and collaborative. When reviewing the current state of journalism and where it is heading we can identify one specific trend that will grow in the journalistic field—collaboration and collaborative technology tools that will help the journalist in the newsgathering, reporting and presentation of the news.

Collaboration in simple terms is the ability to join together toward the completion of a task, activity or process. It incorporates shared responsibilities, participative decision-making, an open system, and a continual flow of communication and feedback among all involved. Collaboration can include a variety of resources such as technologies, people, systems, and processes. In the news industry, collaboration has only been recognized in recent decades through a digital lens via the inception of peer-to-peer journalism models and collaborative news websites.

The changes happening in today's newsrooms around the world reflect that collaboration among journalists and the use of collaborative technologies will become more common and apparent. Why? Because communication and work within and between different departments of journalists, editors, and the public will no longer be isolated but open to all inside and outside the organization. This entails a much higher level of collaboration and cooperation among journalists in the news operation.

Because of this digital and connected environment, people work together on different computers in the same cubicle area, on a different floor, or in different parts of the world. So, the digital workplace will facilitate the ability for multiple journalists to access information and work on it together in the same time and place, making collaboration possible in the workplace and collaborative technology tools a necessity in the 21st century newsroom.

Collaborative technologies will become the future component to daily news tasks. Today, the incorporation of multiple media and equipment requires journalists to think differently about how they cover and report the news. For example, equipment such as video cameras and multimedia applications such as Soundslides and Final Cut Pro are becoming industry standards for journalists around the globe. In a recent survey of online journalists conducted by the Pew Research Center's Project for Excellence in Journalism in conjunction with the Online News Association, of the online journalists surveyed, a large majority said they were using streaming video and audio, podcasts, photo slideshows, mapping, and other interactive formats on their websites to present the news. Another online survey also found online journalists rated knowledge of software applications such as Dreamweaver, multimedia authoring programs and Flash as highly important skills in their newsrooms in addition to the standard journalistic skills of writing and reporting. In a recent article in *American Journalism Review* on the explosion of video online, *Washington Post* officials said they spent a month teaching 12 reporters how to shoot video, *Tampa Tribune* officials said that of the 275 members of their staff, 60 had attended an in-house video training program, and the *Miami Herald* stated it publishes 15 to 18 stand-alone video pieces weekly on its website.

The technological transformation is well underway with journalists embracing these changes in newsgathering, reporting, and presenting the news. Yet there is a challenge. With technology, any technology, learning how it works is not an easy task. In the same Pew survey of online journalists mentioned earlier, 64 percent of journalists surveyed said time was the biggest factor in their impediment to learning new technology in the newsroom. Their lack of interest and workplace attitude factors were ranked lower in comparison, thus demonstrating that tomorrow's journalists are not unwilling to adapt or change—but face a challenge of finding the time and ways of how to incorporate the future technologies into their daily news tasks.

This issue may be alleviated when we think about the form and use of these technologies for the future. These tools will need to become more compatible and versatile for the journalist to easily use for the newsgathering, reporting and presenting of the story. Collaborative technology tools can help to solve this problem.

Collaborative technology tools can be considered items that allow multiple users to access synchronously and asynchronously virtual areas to complete tasks together as a group. When specifically identifying the forms of collaborative technology tools that will have the most influence on the journalist's work in the near future, we can categorize them into three areas: digital communication, mobile management systems, and contextual locators (see figure below). Each of these areas encompasses multiple tools and capabilities allowing the journalist to work in a digital media environment that works off the ingenuity of the journalist.

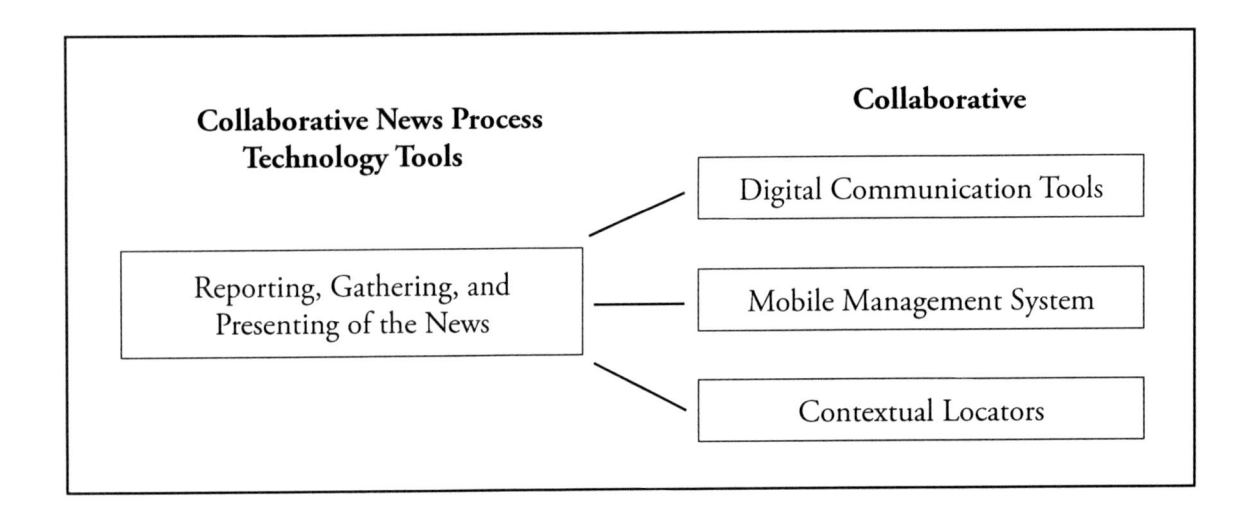

Collaborative News Process Technology Tools

Collaborative

- Reporting, Gathering, and Presenting of the News
  - Digital Communication Tools
  - Mobile Management System
  - Contextual Locators

DIGITAL COMMUNICATION

Digital journalism tools of the future encompass the technologies that support synchronous interaction between individuals and groups despite geographical or physical location. We can identify the early forms of these digital tools, such as Voice Over Internet Protocol (Skype is a popular example) that allows us to converse with one person or several people across the Internet with or without video around the world. In many cases, these forms of communication require that the user has a specific application downloaded to their computer (e.g. Skype, MSN chat, etc.), access to the tool via the cloud (e.g. Google chat) or via physical phone lines. The user must use separate communication tools for communicating for certain tasks or with specific individuals.

Communication is more than ever a vital part of the journalist's work. The use of email, face-to-face conversations and the telephone remain important communication tools. However, the incorporation of wireless technologies along with mobile devices that contain specific applications will open up this realm of what digital communication will be. We are just now beginning to see how the role of text and video chat is being used in newsrooms for conversations, budget meetings, and for clarifying or correcting facts in a news story. This is just the tip of the iceberg in terms of what digital communication is yet to be.

As mentioned earlier with our case of Samantha the journalist, we can envision that the digital communication tools she will use will allow her to instantaneously connect with her editor, producer, designer, videographer and other journalists at the same time with a click of her device. The connection will not be hampered by geographic location and will be voice or video or combination thereof. In addition, the ability to communicate with other users at the same time while exchanging multiple resources (documents, maps, video or audio clips, etc.) with each other will be common as part of the communication stream. These tools of digital communication can be combined as a unified communication platform such as receiving voicemails through email while bringing up a voice or video chat while using the same tool.

MOBILE MANAGEMENT SYSTEMS

Mobile management system tools are the future content management systems for individuals, groups and companies. With the inception of cloud computing and wireless access to systems in the future, the ability for the journalist to access the newsroom's content management system to upload a story, blog, multimedia package or Flash interactive piece will be done with a few clicks from a mobile device anywhere, anytime. The access to these systems will be simultaneous, allowing multiple journalists to access the story at the same time to make modifications and changes on the fly.

Newsroom content management systems are mainly proprietary systems that are specifically created for the news organization and often separated into distinct areas. In many cases, there is a content management system for video, another system for print, another system for the website, another system for user-generated content, and so forth. Confusion wreaks havoc with these multiple content management systems and the complications of learning each system makes it a nightmare for the journalist. In addition, many of today's content management systems are tied to specific IT hardware and software that not only cost the news organization significant money to maintain but also tie down the journalist through the limited locations of access.

Thus, mobile management systems will serve as the future of the content management system for the news operation. In the coming years, the increasing amount of news content that will need to be posted and presented across various media platforms throughout the day, minute-by-minute, will impact the data capacity and bandwidth of these existing management systems making the mobile management system a necessity. No longer will the content be housed on one particular server but across several to meet the robust needs of news produced in the 21st century. In addition, the mobile management systems will be accessible via remote locations from a variety of devices allowing journalists to upload their news stories (despite the media type or platform) to the system while out in the field.

Samantha, our journalist mentioned earlier in the chapter, can log in into her mobile management system and compose her story including maps, blog posts from the public, and audio interviews from rally participants. She can even lay it out accordingly so that her news story can be presented on the website, the digital screen (whether television or computer), and for the mobile device—seamlessly from one system.

CONTEXTUAL LOCATORS

Contextual locators are the tools that provide additional information and resources to journalists as they go about their newsgathering and reporting. These locators may include libraries of primary source information, maps, directories, databases and other relevant resources that journalists can pull up as they are on location and connect it to their stories accordingly. As part of the contextual locator, it will have information and accurate representations that can be a combination of contributions from other individuals such as other journalists, media companies and perhaps even the public, as a way to help fill in any missing pieces. The locators will be able to be updated from anywhere, making it a vital component to journalists' work in the future.

In today's newsrooms, databases are set up to house a variety of archived information and data. Internal library systems or morgues contain old stories, and multimedia libraries may also exist. There is also the news website with pages of information journalists can use for newsgathering—in all of these cases, much of this information is in separate locations and not connected. Journalists often have to go through several channels and resources to find these forms of information, which makes a part of the newsgathering and reporting process more complicated and disjointed. Contextual locators can help this problem. For example, the locator can include a database of articles over the past 50 years from the news organization, a series of archived maps, and various multimedia resources (e.g. audio interviews and transcripts) to help journalists identify the information they may need to use or reference in a part of a story.

THE PUBLIC BENEFIT: JOE, THE 21ST CENTURY NEWS CONSUMER

Each of these three areas demonstrates its potential for the journalist's work, and can also impact the public. Just as we mentioned our future journalist Samantha, we cannot forget the future news consumer as well, Joe. He is a news consumer of the 21st century and often reads Samantha's work, including her coverage of the rally. When Joe receives the first headline and post from Samantha about the rally from his mobile device, he knows the basics of the story. Shortly thereafter, he is notified on his device that he can now view a map of the rally's location, helping him decide if he wants to attend the event or avoid it altogether.

As the day passes, Joe receives more news and information about the rally as Samantha and other journalists post information to the news platform. Joe has read additional posts from people in his community about the rally, has listened and watched a few interviews from the event, and has looked at additional links related to the rally. He wants to see all aspects and layers of the story. As the evening approaches, Joe looks at his digital screen at home to see the news platform to get more news about the rally. He views some video interviews and comments posted by rally participants. He looks at some historical information on previous rallies held in the city, and reviews a wiki calendar that shows when the next series of rallies will be held. Joe illustrates how news consumption by the public will be different and how it will evolve in this century.

Recent surveys have shown that the public is not accessing less news but seeking and receiving more of it via various platforms that include multiple media on a daily basis. The public's news consumption is becoming more widespread and more dispersed. In the coming century, news consumers like Joe and others in the public will continue to expect more from their news organizations and journalists. As Kovach and Rosenstiel stated in *The Elements of Journalism: What Newspeople Should Know and the Public Should Expect,* there is a greater need than ever in the 21st century for journalists to make sense of all the information out there as synthesizers of information so the public can make the informed decisions they need to in their daily lives. Joe and other news consumers like him will not be satisfied with the status quo and will want more layers and context to the news and information they receive.

The collaborative technology tools addressed in this chapter will help the journalist in establishing a stronger connection to the public by how they are able to converse, interact, synthesize, and contextualize the information they are receiving. As a result, the implications of these future collaborative technology tools can help to create an informed society whose members are more aware of their local and global community so they can take specific actions and make decisions accordingly. However, as with any prediction, it is dependent on how much the public embraces these new forms journalism that will determine how effectively these collaborative technology tools will be able to share information with the public.

A FUTURE FOR THE NEWS INDUSTRY?

Recent reports bemoan the future and call for sweeping changes as newspaper circulation rates continue to decline and papers go under, evening national news broadcasts struggle to maintain viewers, and radio wonders how to attract listeners who increasingly opt to plug in their MP3 player instead of switching on a station.

Indeed, the current numbers give one pause to consider if there can be a future for journalists in an industry that seems to be dying. Fewer daily and weekly newspapers exist now than a decade ago, and in terms of personnel, newspapers are faring poorly. Industry magazines reported more than 20,000 jobs were lost industry-wide in 2008, and the Paper Cuts blog tracking layoffs and buyouts at newspapers found a similar number. The Project for Excellence in Journalism in 2009 reported about one in five journalists working in newspapers in 2001 is now gone. "How bad are things in the newspaper business?" Paul Farhi asked in *American Journalism Review*. "So bad that it's newsworthy when a newspaper isn't cutting staff, chopping its newshole or taking some other action that requires another of those ominous Message to Our Readers announcements."

News workers in radio face daunting prospects as well. Radio stations consistently are broadcasting less news and are cutting staff sizes, according to the Radio Television Digital News Association. Fewer than 13,500 people were working in radio at the time of the latest *American Journalist* survey, and their numbers have steadily declined since the survey began. Many of those who work in radio are expected to do more and wear many hats; news directors oversee news production for an average of 3.3 radio stations and more than three-quarters of them said their jobs entail tasks not related to news, according to RTDNA's 2006 study.

Television journalists are also seeing their numbers shrink, nationally and locally. The national networks as well as local stations are cutting their staffs in certain areas, the Project for Excellence in Journalism found in 2008. Although many local stations reported bigger budgets, that was not reflected in adding personnel or increasing salaries. Instead, the additional funds went to technology expenses. Technology also played a role at the national level, especially with the networks expanding their international bureaus. ABC and NBC each had 16 overseas news offices and CBS had 14—increases across the board compared to their numbers a few years ago. But these are not the multi-person bureaus of the past. Thanks to technology that is more advanced and portable, about half of the network bureaus are one-person operations, with that person acting as reporter, editor and producer, according to the Project's State of the Media report.

This rise in the emphasis on technology as a journalist's tool means that technology is transforming the industry on many fronts—the way journalists do their jobs, how they are expected to do their jobs, and where they do them—and shaping what will become of the news industry.

CHANGES IN TECHNOLOGY

With so much pessimism about the state of the news business and dire forecasts for those who work in it, we are left wondering, "How did we get here?" Explanations come from a variety of sources and range from allegations that the corporate mentality of making money at all costs has corroded journalism's dedication to the craft and the production of quality products, as well as claims that the public has abandoned the news—at least in the traditional sense—in favor of other forms of entertainment.

For the professional journalist, the "how did we get here" head-scratching can be addressed with a review of the advances in technology that have revolutionized the newsroom and transformed the journalists in it. Chief among these advances is the adoption of the internet, not only in the newsroom but throughout society, and the changes that hinge upon it. These changes include an increased emphasis on visuals throughout the news industry and the development of devices whose use was spawned by the popularity of the Internet as a news-sharing platform.

THE ALL-POWERFUL INTERNET

The internet has changed communication patterns worldwide and profoundly affected the way journalists perform their jobs and the way they will continue to do them. As the demand for online news grew in the 1990s and news organizations struggled with how to present their products in this new format, journalists began incorporating the web into their job routines—reporters used email to contact sources and gather background information, editors fact-checked stories, and photographers shared digital images and videos. The benefits were straightforward: the ease with which these tasks could be done saved journalists time and made their jobs a little easier. But challenges also arose. The internet became a crutch for some who relied on it as a primary source of information for stories; they took for granted that everything on the internet was true and accurate. Even today, journalists can be drawn in and duped. Take, for instance, the case of MSNBC in late 2007 when it published an article on its website about football star Michael Vick's involvement in a dog-fighting ring. The article quoted the Rev. Al Sharpton, citing the quote as coming from his personal blog. Unfortunately, the blog wasn't Sharpton's, but was instead produced by the newsgroper.com site as a parody. Although this is an extreme example, it illustrates a dangerous position for journalists. Another byproduct of the "convenience" of electronic reporting is the ease with which personal interaction with sources can be replaced by electronic communication, often email. Journalism scholars and practitioners alike have warned of the pitfalls of such contact, namely that the journalist doesn't really know if the person intended is the one sending the response and that allowing the source to construct his or her answers in a written message eliminates spontaneous elements that make for "good journalism." In essence, the journalist is no longer in control of the conversation.

By no means should this be taken as a call to abandon the internet as a journalistic tool—the internet is a vital means of gathering and verifying information and communicating with others. The web truly represents the future of the industry and its professionals. But we must be wary of over-reliance on it—it cannot replace the rapport that is built with face-to-face interaction with sources and colleagues. In addition, the speediness that is a cornerstone of the online experience now has some journalists balking. Myrow, the radio journalist who embarked on her career as the internet was arriving in newsrooms, is concerned with the expectations that the internet sets for journalists. Editors accustomed to the lightning-fast delivery available online demand their reporters produce stories with incredible turnaround. "If the mayor makes an announcement, shouldn't the reporter be able to summarize the what, when, where, how and why on the spot?" Myrow says, explaining editors' mindsets. "There are problems with these presumptions. If a reporter is unfamiliar with the context of the issue, she may not be able to identify the mayor's lies and/or mischaracterizations. There's more than one reason why reporters call 'experts' and 'the other side.' We are often learning the story ourselves as we craft the package we deliver to listeners later in the day. Otherwise, listeners are getting the mayor's press conference unfiltered. The reporter is serving as the tool of the newsmaker, not an advocate for the news consumer," she argues.

Other journalists have experienced struggles with the internet and management. For Mariel Garza at the *Los Angeles Daily News*, one frustration has been getting management to maintain its support of online ventures. "In our opinion section, we had recently started an op-ed blog, called Friendly Fire, in which we have daily opinions from the editorial board as well as our regular columnists. It was quite lively and was starting to make real gains in hits," she says, adding that the paper had encouraged workers to create news-related blogs and enjoyed an increase in online readership and paid print subscriptions. Then, the bottom fell out. "We lost one third of the editorial department staff in layoffs. As a result, the once-thriving blog is withering and dying as the remaining staff—which is so small I'm embarrassed to even say—is scrambling just to put together a decent page and has little time to blog anymore. That's sad, and it's indicative of how corporate management in this business, and at companies across the land, is shooting itself in the foot."

This situation illustrates how media managers, standing at the precipice of the future, are at a loss as how to proceed. Do they step off boldly and risk a stumble that may mean profit loss, or do they plod forward clinging to the old ways and hoping they will somehow rediscover the success they once enjoyed? Linder, who embraced the internet as a reporting tool in its infancy, does not look to management to set the standard for what journalism will become. "Properties like Berserkistan, YouTube, MySpace, FlyTunes and other breakthrough media are rarely born in corporate tar pits where executives are big on copying, acquiring or buying-out, but rarely known for innovation. The big ideas will never happen there thanks to fear, caution, and corporate mindset," he explains.

Looking ahead, the internet's importance as a means of communication for journalists will only intensify. With today's 24/7 news cycle, journalists of every genre rely on the internet to disseminate breaking news. Explains television reporter Kate Weidaw: "Management knows we can't wait for the 5 or 6 p.m. news to show a big story. When it happens, it has to get on the web. We get so excited when we've beaten the competition on a story when it comes to putting it on our website." In many cases, it's not just the big stories that go online first. Any story gets posted before it airs on a newscast.

RISE OF DIGITAL MEDIA

A result of the reliance on the internet in the news business is the emphasis on visual presentation that has grown from it. Television has always been a visual-heavy medium, and magazines and newspapers have relied on photographs to help tell stories. As these organizations, as well as radio, have developed their online platforms, visuals have become increasingly important and will continue to be so. The news isn't presented in the same way it once was. Many of today's news consumers expect multiple elements—they want words, written and spoken, as well as still photos and live video, in a package, and they want ways to interact with their media. They want to contribute their information, their thoughts, their photos, and their video. Advances in digital technology allow them to do this, and have changed how journalists approach their jobs.

It used to be, at least at larger-circulation newspapers, that reporters would specialize on a specific task (writing) on a specific subject (their beat). This is still the core of their job, but now they are also learning to think about their stories beyond words. In the past, they might ask to assign a photographer to shoot an event or arrange a portrait of a newsmaker. Today, the reporter may take along a digital camera or recorder, shooting stills or taping the interview and then linking it from the online publication of the story or posting it to a blog. "Newspaper reporters don't generally think of their stories in a visual or aural way, but we've had to do that to remain competitive," says Garza, the editorial page editor at the *Los Angeles Daily News*. "We've done this by training and encouraging all editorial staffers, not just reporters, to learn how to use digital cameras for short films and recording equipment to make podcasts of good stories. We've had great success with our multimedia packages and we see that as the future."

Not all print journalists have had such positive experiences with their companies' push to incorporate digital technology into their online publications. Nuri Vallbona, who worked as a photojournalist at the *Miami Herald* before taking a buyout, was handed a video recorder and user's manual and asked to shoot video on her assignments. The first day she took the camera, it didn't record the footage she thought she shot. Since then, the paper has instituted better training and shuffled some of its photographers to focus on adding video to its website. "It's been difficult," Vallbona says. "They've taken away four positions to do exclusive video, and added more work for the rest of us. We've had videographers who are working long hours—it's a long and tedious process. It's 18-hour days. The managers making these decisions have not a clue about the video editing process. They just want the end result and don't realize what it takes to get there."

Print media also has had more catching up to do in terms of visual and multimedia presentation, compared to television. For television news personnel, as well as radio, advances in technology have resulted in smaller, more portable reporting and editing systems that enable journalists to work from almost anywhere. For Los Angeles radio field reporter Pete Demetriou, that has meant filing reports from the Gulf War in 1991 with then-new satellite phones because it was the fastest way to relay information, if not the clearest. It meant going live from his Bronco on the side of the freeway moments after the Northridge earthquake in 1994. "I called in and they said, 'Stand by, you're live in 10 seconds,'" he explains, relating how he had been driving home after covering a late-night police standoff when his SUV began bouncing on the road. " I was the first voice many Angelinos heard 15 seconds after the shaking stopped." Today, he and many broadcast reporters are self-contained units, with a laptop for script writing and digital editing and a mobile internet broadband system that connects through what he refers to as a "super-improved cell phone."

While all of these improvements have allowed journalists to get the news out faster, they are not without their pitfalls. Having the technology to produce on-site news reports does not equal good reporting, nor does it equal better ratings or circulation. The majority of the most popular reports on some of the nation's top newspapers' websites are text-only stories and still-photograph galleries, not videos. Vallbona, the *Miami Herald* photojournalist, says this was the case at the paper and a source of contention between managers and staffers. "[Managers think] all think that video is the end-all. They don't realize the YouTube audiences are looking for the best video. Your video might not be that good. It's about quality, not quantity," she explains, adding that online site visitors were hampered by slow download times for videos.

On a typical day, fewer than 20% of adult internet users watch or download online videos and of those who do, not all of them are watching news footage. Not surprisingly, young adults are more active downloaders, but they're not watching news video as frequently as their older counterparts. The good news is that the number of Americans with high-speed internet connections at home or work is rising, and two-thirds of those who have such access have watched or downloaded online videos. As more people gain access to broadband and other high-speed internet sources, video downloads will likely become more popular.

CHANGES IN NEWSROOM STRUCTURE

The internet and technology have redefined how journalists do their jobs and where they do them. No longer are journalists tied to the newsroom, and more and more of them are getting out of the brick-and-mortar buildings. They are in "newsrooms" of their own making, with a few essential tools like a laptop and cell phone. The advances being made in mobile technology enable users to shoot video and photos with their cell phones and special software, to edit those materials and email them back to the office or post them to a website. They are roving reporters writing their stories, compiling photographs, editing video and audio tracks, and posting it on the internet.

Because of the freedom gained with mobile technology, fewer people need to be in the office to do their jobs, and the office needs fewer people to physically put out a product. Demand has gone up in the industry for jack-of-all-trades journalists who can do a bit of everything from anywhere, but we must consider where this will take us.

'BLOWING UP' THE NEWSROOM

Radio and television reporters have been out of the newsroom for quite some time, able to broadcast live from the scene as long as it was within range of their stations' transmitter towers. They still had to go back to the office to produce packages that weren't live, using in-house computers to type a script before handing it off to a supervisor and working from editing systems that were too cumbersome to be mobile. Newspaper journalists have toiled for decades in the newsroom, hammering away on a keyboard before sending the story to an editor, who then turned it over to the page designer. Reporters and photographers might be gone gathering material during the day but would be back in the office to meet deadline. Today, all journalists are less reliant on the cords—literally the ones that supply power to their equipment and connect them to the internet—that used to keep them in the office. Soon those cords will be relics of the past. The newsroom as it once was will be irrelevant.

Traditionalists may cling to the notion that the newsroom is a place where everyone must come to work but that's not reality. With the right equipment, journalists can work anywhere. Smart media companies are starting to recognize this but have stopped short of embracing it. One stumbling block is money—as they work to maintain the high profit margins they formerly enjoyed, media corporations are reluctant to dole out any more cash than absolutely necessary. They see technology as helping journalists do their jobs, but not crucial to it. They fail to see how using technology to "free" their workers from the newsroom will enliven their product and make it better, and more profitable.

The future of the newsroom is to blow it up. Start with a blank slate and look at who *has* to be there. Reporters and photographers in print and broadcast alike spend most of their time outside the office. With the internet's introduction of the 24-hour news cycle, the need for their attention to be directed outside the office at all hours is even greater. They don't usually arrive in the office until they are done with their assignments for the shift and come back to write and/or edit them. They spend their time at a computer compiling their material and sending it up the line. These workers—the laborers of the journalism world—are also the easiest ones to move out of the newsroom.

Some companies have recognized this, as Garza of the *Daily News* explains: "We're blogging from home or from our laptops during a meeting or from the scene of a crime. We're reporting on our cell phones in our cars or from our living rooms."

Reporters and photographers may still come in to meet with supervisors and collaborate with coworkers, but in the future they won't be familiar faces in the newsroom. They will be known by the digital files they send in that contain their work. It makes more business sense to have reporters out in the field, gathering news—that's the commodity of our business. We trade in information. If the workers can work from the field more often, it makes them more likely to be able to cover more news.

Since money speaks to the people who make the decisions that set the course of the industry's future, let's start with the dollars. One of the single largest expenses in any organization is its people and having a place to put them. As we've already seen, technology increases efficiency and eliminates the need for certain jobs. Giving a reporter a laptop, a cell phone, and a broadband card, for example, allows that person to stay in the field longer, getting more information or covering additional stories. If the reporter doesn't have to come into the office to file his or her stories, that's a little less space that's needed in the newsroom. Fewer people in the newsroom translates to less money being spent on a lot of other necessities, like office supplies and electricity. Money is also saved in paying mileage for workers who use their own vehicles to get from assignment to assignment and then back to the office. By allowing them to work from location, companies can save money.

Another benefit to moving reporters and photographers out of the newsroom is to make happier reporters and photographers. Among journalists' chief complaints about their jobs are the long hours and lack of autonomy. Enabling workers to work from outside the office will cut down on the time they are forced to spend shuttling between the office and assignments and raise their perception of the amount of control they feel they have over the execution of their jobs. Both of these issues, when left unsatisfied, lead to lowered job satisfaction, job burnout, and eventual job turnover. The industry struggles to retain workers, especially women and minorities, and changes to grant them greater satisfaction will help stem the flow of those opting to turn in their press credentials.

THE ALL-IN-ONE JOURNALIST

We live in an era in which anyone with something to say can express those thoughts to the masses with the right equipment. At the most basic level, all that is needed is access to a computer connected to the internet. From there, anyone can create a blog. But most news consumers expect more—they want visuals and sound to go with their words. Enter the video camera and basic editing software that can cut together a digital package. Whether this ability makes the producer a journalist is an ongoing debate and is discussed in another chapter. What it does mean is that anyone who considers himself or herself a journalist must keep learning and applying new skills.

Professional journalists and journalism educators seem to agree on the basic skills needed for a career in news: good interviewing, solid reporting, talented writing, and ethical reasoning. Journalism schools are expanding their multimedia and convergence training based on reports from graduates and other professionals who say that expertise is in demand. About half of the students leaving journalism schools have had classes that included writing and editing stories for online publication, according to Pew data. These numbers will continue to climb because online proficiency is required for so many jobs. Online skills are important to those doing the hiring, especially at larger newspapers where online reporting skills top the list of things editors are looking for in a new hire. The technical skill sets that once delineated between print and broadcast journalists are blending as more companies merge and consolidate, and expand their products to include "new" sources of news. Now, industry-wide expectations dictate staffers be able to write print, broadcast and online versions of the same story, and be prepared to produce a multimedia package of that information.

As journalist Linder explains: "Increasingly, the medium no longer matters." News often looks the same across newspaper, television, and radio websites and journalists need to be able to fit into any of these markets. "The roving reporter will become the norm and, thankfully, miniaturization of audio and video recording devices and smaller mobile computers … will turn today's backpack journalists into reporters who can file across most any medium with handheld gear," Linder says. This go-anywhere capability is what will attract the audience with better storytelling and powerful reporting if journalists can provide context for their readers, listeners, and viewers. "In modern journalism, you need to have personal experience, know areas you're talking about. There's no substitute for seeing what's going on and being able to translate to people what's going on," says Demetriou, who works in news radio.

A negative side effect emerges from the popularity of jack-of-all trade journalists. Companies looking to cut costs see these employees as ones who can "do it all" and opt to cut specialized positions. At some stations, newsroom budget cuts have meant replacing trained specialists with ever-smaller and cheaper new devices. Instead of sending a reporter and photographer to shoot a story, just the reporter will go. "They like to call them backpack journalists," says television reporter Weidaw. She concedes that digital technology has made it easier to be a "one-man band," but that it's not necessarily better. "What it really means is we're going to pay you less to do more work and expect just as good quality. What ends up happening are TV stations are hiring more young and inexperienced journalists who then put on a product that is not as good as a seasoned journalist or one with a photographer."

Like it or not, the one-person reporter/editor/photographer/producer "team" is becoming a staple of journalism and is part of the industry's future. We can expect to see journalists—as well as anyone with a story to tell and the skills to operate a video camera and edit the footage—reporting from near and far. This will increase the quantity of news available, but not necessarily the quality. Readers and viewers will be able to depend on us for the "what," as in what's happening around the world, but less often the "why." It is cheaper for corporate media to send one person to cover a story, even though that person is likely to be spread thin by the demands of technology. Whereas he or she once had to research a story and develop questions, that person now also has to set up shots and lighting, write the story/script, edit the package, and post it online—usually on the same deadline as when just the story was required. Websites like angryjournalist.com are littered with journalists frustrated by the demands of their jobs. They lash out at all the responsibility heaped upon them in an effort to keep up with the competition as their colleagues are laid off. Technology has enabled us to add bells and whistles to journalism that make it *look* better, but the vexing dilemma for the future is using those tools to make journalism more meaningful.

GOING FORWARD

Journalists today look different than their predecessors—they are not weighed down by unwieldy equipment or as constrained by the limits of reporting from remote locations. Their "offices" fit in a bag. These mobile journalists work with smaller, speedier equipment that allows them to connect to the web from almost anywhere in the world. It has and will continue to reconfigure the news industry, making the physical newsroom an unnecessary stop on the road of information dissemination. Backpack journalists will dominate the business, proficient in the skills once reserved for those who defined themselves as print or broadcast journalists and masters of adapting the craft to fit the public's constant demand for online information. Says radio reporter Myrow: "I picture the reporter of the future looking something like a Terminator. Video camera strapped to forehead. Voice-operated edit commands. The final product is found on blogs, either by topic or the blogger's personality." Creating an identity the public can identify will be crucial, agrees fellow radio journalist Linder. "As media boundaries dissolve, radio station, television station, newspaper or blog identities will no longer be relevant. What will matter is brand identity: End-users will gravitate to content based on their trust of an established journalism brand, be it the *New York Times* or Daily Kos."

The old genre of news printed on a page versus heard on the radio versus seen on television is giving way to the public's demand for information available on a variety of platforms. Online access to news and other information will be the main mode of delivery as more and more households get high-speed internet access. This can already be seen in the sweeping changes of America's newsrooms. The internet has reshaped how journalists do their jobs as well as how their stories are presented to the audience. In many ways, the web has been a boon to journalists by allowing them to work more efficiently and effectively. But those benefits have been soured by challenges like the expectation of quick turnaround on news. "Just because you can get pictures of a protest online immediately doesn't mean the public has a greater understanding of what's going on, especially if the public doesn't have any understanding of what's going on in the bigger scheme of things around the protest," Myrow explains. Her concerns illustrate one of the pitfalls journalists will face in the future—many sources will provide news to the audience but because of the desire to be "first" with the information, fewer news organizations will focus on explaining and analyzing the news.

Writer Tim Rutten suggested a solution for this dilemma at newspapers, and it can be applied to other media as they struggle with the paths to follow for their online and "traditional" offerings. He believes the future of newspapers is to create "a hybrid publication in which an online edition that's focused mainly on breaking news and service works in tandem with a print edition whose staples are analysis, context and opinion. The former almost surely will have a lot more video and interactivity than it does today; the latter will have to be much more thoughtful and far more intensely and carefully edited." The Gannett Co. launched a venture similar to this suggestion in 2006 and 2007 at its newspapers, whose newsrooms were reorganized into divisions that focus on developing local news and public journalism projects, inviting community contributions, increasing user-generated content, and getting it all online as quickly as possible in a variety of platforms. It turned away from separating its workers into the traditional national, metro, and sports departments to create these new desks. Media corporations, which have been able to acquire newspapers and television and radio stations in the same market, will use Gannett's model in the future and move it forward. Companies won't orient their structure based on whether the end products will appear in print or on broadcast channels; instead, those multiple holdings will be merged into a single digital method of delivery. Mobile journalists will produce their stories in the field and submit these packages, which will contain written as well as audio and video components, to editors who will post them onto the corporation's website. The site will act as an online clearinghouse for users to watch, read, or download onto their medium of choice. News and information won't be identified as coming from a certain newspaper or television station but from a media company.

Several research and development efforts have been made by specific news organizations in recent years that show where the places of innovation for the news industry are developing. These R&D efforts include the work of the *New York Times*. Since 2007, it has developed new ways and forms of presenting news and information to the public via personalization features on the website, presentation and access options of news from the mobile device, and recent experiments with e-readers. They continue to innovate and inform the public of projects and experiments via the First Look blog.

Internationally, Al-Jazeera recently developed its R&D efforts, exploring new forms of presenting news and information to the public internationally through experiments with RSS feeds, podcasts and using the Ushahidi, an open-source platform to help crowdsource information about conflicts in the Middle East by using it to map the conflict in Gaza. Al-Jazeera continues to explore new channels of experimentation with recent content partnerships set up with mobile providers in the Middle East. There is also the recent effort of the BBC Learning Open Lab that allows anyone from the community to view and test prototypes the media organization is creating for educational purposes. In addition, BBC Journalism Labs launched in early 2009. Its blog features the latest and greatest innovations they are working on such as accessing the news via mobile devices and using map radar for news.

These are just a few examples of the research and development efforts taking off at a select number of news organizations around the world. R&D departments in the news industry are not new but its purpose died shortly after the failed news experiments of the 1970s with videotext. However, the R&D effort has now been rejuvenated in the news industry for the 21st century with new technologies and innovations on the horizon to be explored and experimented with.

Today's efforts, as mentioned in the previous pages, serve as a small example of the innovation and change yet to come for journalism. The efforts we discussed in this chapter, and those still to come from future news innovations, will show us how collaborative technology tools will form.

Naysayers are fond of predicting that journalism is an industry on its way out because the public's appetite for news is dwindling. What is really happening is that the public's taste for news and the way they want to receive it is changing—the audience is no longer satisfied to passively receive the news at times the media dictates. They want their news and information now, on their terms. Journalists must adjust to the new world of news delivery by altering their work routines and expanding their skill sets to integrate themselves into the new world. In summary, the full profile of Samantha the journalist mentioned earlier in this chapter demonstrates the potential future of journalism—when the collaborative technology tools of digital communication, mobile management systems, and contextual locators are embraced by the journalist and used to help in the newsgathering, reporting and presenting of the news story to the public and news consumers like Joe, resulting in a new form of 21st century journalism.

SUGGESTED READING

McLellan, Michele & Porter, Tim (2007). *News, improved: How America's newsrooms are learning to change.* Washington, D.C.: CQ Press.

Stepp, Carl Sessions (2008, April/May.) Maybe it is time to panic. *American Journalism Review 30 (2)*, 22-27.

Sylvie, George & Witherspoon, Patricia (2002). *Time, change and the American newspaper.* Mahwah, NJ: Lawrence Erlbaum.

Weaver, David, Beam, Randal, Brownlee, Bonnie, Voakes, Paul, and Wilhoit, G.Cleveland (2007). *The American journalist in the 21st century: U.S. news people at the dawn of the new millennium.* Mahwah, N.J.: Lawrence Erlbaum.

Witschge, Tamara & Nygren, Gunnar (2009). Journalistic work: A profession under pressure? *Journal of Media Business Studies, 6(1),* 37-59.

Chapter 5

Citizen Journalism: Motivations, Methods, and Momentum

Seth C. Lewis

If THE CITIZEN JOURNALISM phenomenon emerging in the early 21st century had a turning point, or simply a moment befitting our postmodern milieu, perhaps it occurred here: at a rather ordinary event in the middle of an otherwise unordinary U.S. presidential campaign. As the Democratic Party nomination battle between Barack Obama and Hillary Rodham Clinton slogged through the spring of 2008, headed toward an uncertain endgame in the summer, Obama supporters gathered for a private fundraiser in San Francisco. April 6 was a quiet Sunday, a lull between primaries. This invitation-only evening affair, hosted at a mansion in the Pacific Heights neighborhood, would be Obama's fourth fundraiser of the day. It was closed to the press. But it wasn't closed to Mayhill Fowler.

This was hardly unusual. As a blogger for OffTheBus.net, a network of unpaid writers and researchers covering the presidential campaign for the Huffington Post website, Fowler was a regular at Obama fundraisers and had blogged about them before. Indeed, she herself was an Obama supporter, having maxed out at $2,300 in contributions. So the campaign figured it had little to fear from this former homemaker and Obama loyalist—who also happened to be a rising-star citizen journalist. For journalist she had become. This 61-year-old with time and money on her hands had developed quite a following on the Huffington Post with her highly reflective style of reporting, in which candidate quotes often appeared buried in her blog posts, wrapped inside layers of contextual (and personal) narrative. "It violates almost all of the conventions of traditional reporting (though not its ethical code)," Marc Cooper, editorial director for OffTheBus, would later write, "and that's what makes it all so damn interesting."

As she went to the fundraiser that night, Fowler wasn't expecting much. "I thought maybe I'd find something for background, I thought one sentence, maybe a dependent clause," she told Katharine Q. Seelye of the *New York Times*. And she almost left early when Obama launched into his stump speech, one she knew well from the campaign trail; she had just finished tailing Obama around Pennsylvania—but in a separate car, not on the campaign bus. Plus, the house was hot and stuffy, packed with semi-wealthy Californians clamoring to capture the event with their cell phone and video cameras. But then, with her digital recorder poised, Fowler heard something that took her aback. In the now-famous remarks, Obama, in describing the economic plight of rural Americans, said, "It's not surprising then they get bitter, they cling to guns or religion or antipathy to people who aren't like them or anti-immigrant sentiment or anti-trade sentiment as a way to explain their frustrations."

Fowler knew this was newsworthy but spent days stewing over what to do about it, torn by conflicting loyalties to the campaign and to her readers, and worried that whatever she wrote would be torn out of context. "There are no standards of journalism on the internet," she later told Seelye. "I'm always second-guessing myself. Is this the right thing to do? Am I being fair?" Five days later, on a Friday (fewer people would see it that way, she reasoned), after consulting with Huffington Post editors, she published her report, though with the lightning quote couched inside several paragraphs of ruminations.

The post immediately hit the fan, generating 250,000 hits and 5,000 comments within 48 hours. It became global news within hours, and the "bitter" quote and its fallout dominated much of the headlines leading up to the Pennsylvania primary later that month. In a new era of YouTube politics—in which virtually no candidate appearance or public utterance goes unrecorded, amplifying the impact and potential of the "gotcha" snippet as well as the full-length speech—Fowler's work was as apposite as it was influential: another case of the internet changing politics and its mediation through the press.

"I'm 61," Fowler told the *New York Times*. "I can't believe I would be one of the people who's changing the world of media."

And so we come to the central question of this chapter: Is all of this—this citizen journalism, this mixing and melding of amateur and professional in news production, this opportunity for seemingly anyone to inform and influence on a massified scale—really changing media? In our attention-deficit news cycle, "Bittergate" caused an instant furor but ultimately lost its flame, rather quickly falling out of the headlines and off the agenda of Sunday morning talk shows, even if its embers burned on for weeks in the hyper-partisan blogosphere. Today, the episode is just one more relic of a supercharged 2008 presidential campaign. And yet, the Fowler case is instructive because it illustrates the essence of citizen journalism: the uncertain, unclear, indeed untidy reconfiguration of roles, causing us to question what exactly *is* news and what qualifies one to report it. Was Fowler a supporter, a blogger, a journalist ... all three, or something else entirely? "We had a fundamental misunderstanding of my priorities," Fowler said at the time, explaining her relationship with the Obama campaign. "Mine were as a reporter, not as a supporter. They thought I would put the role of supporter first."

We're entering new territory here, as New York University professor Jay Rosen likes to remind us. "Citizen journalism isn't a hypothetical in this campaign," Rosen wrote. He was at the vanguard in articulating citizen journalism (and the public journalism movement that preceded it), and helped create OffTheBus.net with Arianna Huffington. "It's not a beach ball for newsroom curmudgeons, either. It's Mayhill Fowler, who had been in Pennsylvania with Obama, listening to the candidate talk about Pennsylvanians to supporters in San Francisco, and hearing something that didn't sound right to her." Rosen and Huffington saw the potential for conflicts with the campaigns as supporters behaved as reporters. "But we also felt that participants in political life had a right to report on what they saw and heard themselves," Rosen wrote on the Huffington Post, "not as journalists claiming no attachments but as citizens *with* attachments who were relinquishing none of their rights."

"Citizen" or "journalist"? Spectator or reporter? New territory indeed. This hybridization of news production threatens to rupture all we've come to understand about delineations between journalist and audience, producer and user, professional and non. Where does newswork end and media consumption begin, particularly when technologies such as the internet increasingly enable and encourage open-source cooperation and information sharing across networks? Where are the defined boundaries as we enter a stage of continuous creation through collaborative communities, moving as we do from traditional production to what media scholar Axel Bruns calls "produsage"? It is at this juncture of convergence, amid slippery distinctions and blurring roles, where content is mashed and repurposed through participatory media, that we examine the future of citizen journalism: How did we get here, and where are we going toward 2020 and beyond?

That's a broad question, of course, and one that could lead down many avenues worth exploring. But for the purposes of this chapter we will first focus on understanding the essence of today's citizen journalism, and then consider three features shaping the future of user-generated news and information:

- *Motivations*—the underlying rationale, on the part of users and producers alike, to embrace citizen journalism;
- *Methods*—the Web 2.0 tools of today and Web 3.0 platforms of tomorrow for facilitating grassroots participation in news creation; and
- *Momentum*—the driving trends of pro-am convergence—across media roles and platforms—that are central to the future of collaborative journalism.

WHAT IS CITIZEN JOURNALISM?

Like other fashionable buzzwords of the digital age, "citizen journalism" is a catch-all term for a number of principles and processes at work. Its parent term is "citizen media," which is often invoked in discussions of another internet buzzword—user-generated content—and its manifold manifestations, from blogs to wikis to social networking. All of this has occurred largely within the framework of Web 2.0, representing not so much a technical change in the internet as a major step forward in software that facilitates collaboration in creating and sharing information (think: photos on Flickr, videos on YouTube, and personal data on Facebook and MySpace). As such, Web 2.0 has spawned a "Generation C" of users, so named because they have new skills and interests in "content" and "creativity," not to mention their contribution to the "casual collapse" of traditional media as well as their ability to generate "cash" from their activities, as Bruns points out. Bruns, himself no stranger to buzzwords (having coined "produsage" to describe the paradigm shift occurring in the producer-consumer relationship in media and beyond), notes that Web 2.0 marks a movement "from static to dynamic content, from hierarchically managed to collaboratively and continuously developed material, and from user-as-consumer to user-as-contributor."

This user-led phenomenon is important for understanding the rise of citizen journalism in the early 21st century. As we'll discuss later, a more open and adaptive internet architecture has provided the means and tapped the motivations for user-generated news to flourish. And, in the future, as computing increasingly becomes a mobile activity, less connected with the desktop paradigm (physically and metaphorically speaking), with user interfaces better suited for content creation and sharing by anyone, anywhere, anytime—then, as now, technology will play a substantial part in shaping the citizen journalism of tomorrow.

But, first, we must conceptualize this present form of journalism, today. Think of it as *news as process* as opposed to *news as product*—perhaps exemplified in the differences between continuously updating web pages and the fixed, unchanging edition of a print newspaper. This isn't to say that all citizen journalism occurs online (though most of it does), but rather that its DNA is better suited to an environment that privileges nonlinear, multi-sourced adaptability over top-down, one-way editorial control.

More importantly, however, citizen journalism is about the people who produce it—you, me, and potentially any one of the 2 billion people carrying camera-equipped cell phones, to name a few. They (or, *we*) are The People Formerly Known as the Audience, to use Jay Rosen's phrase. In a 2006 post of the same name on his PressThink blog, Rosen captured the essence of this shift:

> The people formerly known as the audience are those who *were* on the receiving end of a media system that ran one way, in a broadcasting pattern, with high entry fees and a few firms competing to speak very loudly while the rest of the population listened in isolation from one another—and who *today* are not in a situation like that *at all*.
> - Once they were your printing presses; now that humble device, the blog, has given the press to us. That's why blogs have been called little First Amendment machines. They extend freedom of the press to more actors.
> - Once it was *your* radio station, broadcasting on *your* frequency. Now that brilliant invention, podcasting, gives radio to us. And we have found more uses for it than you did.
> - Shooting, editing and distributing video once belonged to you, Big Media. Only you could afford to reach a TV audience built in your own image. Now video is coming into the user's hands, and audience-building by former members of the audience is alive and well on the web.
> - You were once (exclusively) the editors of the news, choosing what ran on the front page. Now we can edit the news, and our choices send items to our own front pages.
>
> A highly centralized media system had connected people "up" to big social agencies and centers of power but not "across" to each other. Now the horizontal flow, citizen-to-citizen, is as real and consequential as the vertical one.

As Rosen makes clear, however, this doesn't mean Big Media are going to be replaced by We Media. Theatergoers do not storm the stage to put on their own production; they still consume with pleasure. Thus, this tension between legacy media and citizen media is not an *either/or* phenomenon but rather a *both/and* condition of complementary strengths. Big Media and We Media can co-exist (and perhaps even thrive together) because they have different goals and meet different needs. Nonetheless, the audience has served notice, and at least some media executives have gotten the message. Rosen points to this remark from Associated Press CEO Tom Curley, from his remarks to the Online News Association in 2004: "The users are deciding what the point of their engagement will be—what application, what device, what time, what place." As for what this supercharged audience actually *does* to create journalism, Mark Glaser, who writes the MediaShift blog, described it best:

> The idea behind citizen journalism is that people without professional journalism training can use the tools of modern technology and the global distribution of the internet to create, augment or fact-check media on their own or in collaboration with others. For example, you might write about a city council meeting on your blog or in an online forum. Or you could fact-check a newspaper article from the mainstream media and point out factual errors or bias on your blog. Or you might snap a digital photo of a newsworthy event happening in your town and post it online. Or you might videotape a similar event and post it on a site such as YouTube.
>
> All these might be considered acts of journalism, even if they don't go beyond simple observation at the scene of an important event. Because of the wide dispersion of so many excellent tools for capturing live events—from tiny digital cameras to videophones—the average citizen can now make news and distribute it globally, an act that was once the province of established journalists and media companies.

Put this way, citizen journalism is a fairly straightforward concept—the average person creating and distributing news via a global medium. But it often gets lost in translation, both in the professional and academic literature, and it can easily become ill-defined in theory and ill-deployed in practice. Part of the problem begins with the name itself. "Citizen journalism" places newsmaking within the boundaries of national identity, which is problematic, and obscures the fact that professional journalists think and act like "citizens."

That's why Jeff Jarvis, a media consultant famous for his Buzzmachine blog, prefers the term "networked journalism," which, he says, "takes into account the collaborative nature of journalism now: professionals and amateurs working together to get the real story, linking to each other across brands and old boundaries to share facts, questions, answers, ideas, perspectives. It recognizes the complex relationships that will make news. And it focuses on the process more than the product." Regardless, whether it's called "networked journalism," or "grassroots journalism," or something else entirely, the essence remains the same: Journalism is no longer the provenance of professionals only. The door is open, even if only slightly in some cases, for regular folks to *act* in creating news content, as opposed to merely *reacting* to it.

In that vein, perhaps a more appropriate emphasis is *participatory* journalism, because that word captures the core element of user-generated news—active involvement from many parties, not just a production of a single (news) entity. Seen this way, participatory journalism is an extension of what Yale Law professor Yochai Benkler dubbed "commons-based peer production" in his seminal paper "Coase's Penguin, or Linux and the Nature of the Firm." This open-source model of production harnesses and harvests the collective energy and intelligence of large numbers of people, each doing small tasks that contribute to a larger project, and often with little organizational direction and no compensation. It's in this sense that media scholar Mark Deuze and his colleagues defined participatory journalism as "any kind of newswork at the hands of professionals and amateurs, of journalists and citizens, and of users and producers benchmarked by what Benkler calls commons-based peer production."

But even that definition might be somewhat misleading. For while some citizen journalism is open-source in nature (more on "crowdsourcing" later), much of it occurs within institutional, corporate frameworks that allow for content creation and submission, but not the user-level editing of, say, a Wikipedia. So, we consider yet another term: *multiperspectival* journalism. It reflects the varied viewpoints we might expect from such composite participation. This multiperspectival concept was first introduced three decades ago by journalism researcher Herbert Gans. He lamented that mainstream news organizations couldn't (or wouldn't) include a fuller array of community views on the news. He suggested that "the news, and the news media, be multiperspectival, presenting and representing as many perspectives as possible—and at the very least, more than today." He further mused, rather boldly: "It is proper to ask who should be responsible for story selection and production. *The news may be too important to leave to the journalists alone*" (emphasis added).

But how that was to be accomplished, how such multiplicity of views could be aggregated and distributed and ultimately discussed in the public sphere, was beyond Gans' imagination in the late 1970s. A few decades later, all of that would change.

AN ABBREVIATED HISTORY

While there's hardly space in this chapter to consider citizen journalism from beginning to end, a little history is in order. Dan Gillmor, a newspaper columnist turned blogger turned new media advocate, has been *the* leading light in the citizen journalism movement, and his book *We the Media: Grassroots Journalism by the People, for the People* charts the rise of this new form of journalism: from the anonymous pamphleteers during the United States' founding to the citizen-captured video of Rodney King's beating by police in 1991, aided along the way by the telegraph, telephone, and personal computing. With the emergence of the web, so came the possibility for do-it-yourself (DIY) publishing to an increasingly wide, unfiltered audience. The anti-globalization movement in the late 1990s spawned Indymedia to challenge corporate media coverage, just as OhmyNews appeared in 2000 as an alternative to the conservative press in South Korea. This pushback against mainstream media continued and was crystallized with the rise of blogs around the same time. Blogging came into its own on Sept. 11, 2001 and during the war in Iraq, and for many people blogs are still synonymous with citizen journalism—this despite a Pew Research survey found that most bloggers don't think of themselves as journalists nor do they want to behave like one.

Citizen journalism's next and most enduring phase would be *hyperlocal*. As journalism scholar Chris Anderson has noted, by 2005, around the time people realized that blogs were largely dependent on the legacy media for content and did little reporting of their own, we saw the emergence of microlocal journalism. Online news sites (or print/online hybrids) would use contributions from local residents to highlight neighborhoods and issues that went underrepresented by the traditional press. Soon the industry was abuzz over the likes of *The Northwest Voice* in Bakersfield, Calif.; myMissourian.com in Columbia, Mo.; and *Bluffton Today* in South

Carolina. Such outlets depended almost entirely on user-generated content—most of it prosaic (think: photos of pets), yet often popular with locals. Even if such sites tended to open the floodgates to write-ups on school fundraisers and bake sales, as opposed to meatier reporting, their success proved that if an easy-to-use platform were provided, citizen journalists would jump abroad. What's more, Anderson notes, hyperlocal journalism "also solved a business problem, one that it didn't necessarily set out to solve:" It proved that user-generated content could make money.

That revelation set in motion the current love-fest for citizen journalism, as news executives who once saw it as a threat now seize it as the future. It's Old Media meets Web 2.0: Newspapers by the score were opening their websites to comments and contributions during 2006; USA Today was refashioning itself as a social networking destination in 2007; CNN, as if handing over the keys to its internet wheel, was giving users free rein of its new citizen-journalism site in 2008 (iReport's slogan: "Unedited. Unfiltered. News."); and similar efforts are spreading among news organizations large and small as the decade closes.

MOTIVATIONS: WHY CITIZEN JOURNALISM?

This leads us to consider the underlying rationale for citizen journalism, and where all of this is positioned within the larger field of media, society, and polity. Broadly speaking, the forces undergirding participatory journalism could be envisioned as a triangulated interplay of Citizen, Corporate, and Convergence.

The Citizen speaks to the political orientation of the movement: its normative goal of improving democracy by nurturing a more engaged and better-informed citizenry. As early proponents Shayne Bowman and Chris Willis put it in their "We Media" manifesto: "The intent of this participation is to provide independent, reliable, accurate, wide-ranging and relevant information that a democracy requires." The Citizen aspect of this equation also calls to mind the philosophical roots of this phenomenon, extending naturally from the public/civic journalism movement of the 1990s. That earlier effort believed in making journalism more responsive to ordinary people, and in turn helping ordinary people become more active in solving community problems and taking part in politics. Participatory journalism tools and trends—from blogs to wikis to crowdsourcing, as well as enhanced opportunities for the audience to upload its own content and fact-check professionally produced material—have much the same aim. Thus, both civic and citizen journalism pivot off an ideal envisioned by the late James Carey; in a democracy, he believed, journalism should be about helping a community have a conversation with itself. In this way, participatory news holds the promise to fulfill the never-quite-realized vision of public journalism's pioneers. "Unlike in the first phase of public journalism, where news organizations initiated the engagement," wrote public journalism researcher Joyce Nip, "in this second phase, the public themselves hold the possibility of taking the initiative."

Certainly, there are other, non-political reasons for wanting to be a citizen journalist. In a *First Monday* essay called "Constructing a Framework to Enable an Open Source Reinvention of Journalism," Leonard Witt points to various models for motivating people to contribute. One has been around for decades: Every day, journalists persuade sources to give up their time and information, at no cost. Publicists cooperate because it's their job, academics do it for career enhancement, social activists do it for the cause, and others go on record for civic duty or for the hedonistic pleasure of seeing their name in print. Witt also notes that in the free- and open-source software literature similar motivation words pop up: reputation, career benefits, fun, community, and recognition. And what of money? It seems reasonable that if audience members were paid a per-click rate for stories posted or videos uploaded, the quantity (and perhaps quality) of citizen offerings would increase. But, as Witt points out, if the open-source software phenomenon has taught us anything, it's that Yochai Benkler's "sharing nicely" model really works; under the right conditions, people will share, just as they were taught to do on the playground as kids. It's in our DNA to contribute.

The Corporate reminds us that participatory journalism is not entirely bottom-up. Much of it occurs within the parameters and on the platforms established by large media companies, who wield ultimate editorial control in varying degrees, as witnessed by the wide array of models for citizen journalism—from the freewheeling Slashdot to the tightly monitored newspaper forums. As Deuze and his colleagues note:

> The common use of "citizen journalism" as a blanket term for such news publishing models to some extent obscures the significant differences in approach between the various participatory news websites currently in operation. In spite of the involvement of citizens as contributors, some such sites retain a degree of conventional editorial control over what is eventually published, while others publish all submitted content immediately, or allow registered users to vote on what passes through the publication's gates; similarly, some sites harness their communities as content contributors mainly at the response and discussion stage, while others rely more immediately on users as contributors of original stories.

Thus, gatekeeping doesn't disappear with citizen journalism; it just becomes more subtle, depending on who is watching the gates—whether it's YouTube, the *New York Times*, or *Bluffton Today*. Moreover, it's important to know why the Corporate has crashed the citizen journalism party, creating more platforms for participation but also injecting a Big Media element that didn't exist in the early days of Indymedia. The shift began in 2005. With newspapers hemorrhaging readership like never before, publishers began to imagine (wrongly, however) that user-generated content would solve their woes. (*Hey, free labor!*) The industry literature of the time is loaded with 12-step programs for anxious news executives to fire up a citizen media venture. As journalism professor Clyde Bentley and his colleagues at the University of Missouri described the mood, in a case study of their citizen journalism creation, myMissourian.com: "If necessity is the mother of invention, panic may be the mother of journalistic innovation."

Hence was born the Citizen-Corporate hybrid, a bottom-up, top-down mash-up befitting this era of Convergence. MIT professor Henry Jenkins famously defined "convergence culture" as interplay between conflicting and complementary forces: Media companies are becoming savvier in delivering their content more aggressively and more broadly to expand their revenue, even as consumers are learning to bring media content (including news) more fully under their control, to consume it and repurpose it how and when they see fit. Convergence is not merely about technology; it describes a social and cultural shift that's occurring in part because of new media technologies. The result is a participatory culture where traditional and new media mix and meld in unpredictable ways, through processes that are both corporate-driven and grassroots-enabled. Sometimes those forces work symbiotically; other times they are at war with each other. In convergence culture, participation and collaboration is prized, assumptions about production and consumption are challenged, and the resulting change in the way we engage media and popular culture has implications for work, life, play, politics—and journalism.

As we consider citizen journalism today, and imagine the shape it's likely to take in the future, convergence is the unifying force, creating a "third space" between top-down and bottom-up news ventures. Consider the convergence model of *Bluffton Today*, a combination of a free newspaper and a community website serving an affluent region on South Carolina's coast. In their case study of *Bluffton Today*, Deuze and colleagues write:

> What makes the paper and site a prime example of a true hybrid between professional and amateur participatory news is its deliberate choice to have (slightly edited) user-generated content as its prime source of news and information. According to Morris [Publishing Group] analyst Steve Yelvington, *Bluffton Today* is an "experiment in citizen journalism, a complete inversion of the typical online newspaper model," as staffers as well as registered community members get a blog, a photo gallery, read/write access to a shared public community calendar, a community cookbook, and an application that supports podcasting and the uploading of video clips. Regarding the paper, readers' online comments on stories that appear in the print edition are edited and printed in the hard copy of next day's newspaper.

One of the unintended consequences of *Bluffton Today's* beta launch, with its tweaking and tinkering to fit community tastes, was improved transparency and dialogue that translated into greater trust among the community, executives said. Deuze et al. concluded that "convergence culture seems to instill increased levels of transparency in the media system, where producers and consumers of content can 'see' each other at work, as they both play each other's roles."

In sum, the tangled interplay of Citizen, Corporate and Convergence has set the stage for participatory journalism to flourish—but those forces, of course, are only part of the story. To fully examine citizen journalism in the present, and make some prediction about its path, we must reflect on the technology that got us here, and envision a few tools that might emerge in the future.

METHODS: TOOLS OF TODAY, TOOLS OF TOMORROW

Blogs. Wikis. Podcasts. YouTube. Twitter. That new media have been central to the rise of participatory news, offering easy platforms for creation and publication, goes without saying. Yet, it's important to remember that these tools—from the free Web 2.0 software to the increasingly cheap hardware afforded by digital cameras and low-cost computers—are "new" only in a relative sense. Each epoch has seen what Roger Fidler calls "mediamorphosis"—an evolution, more than revolution, from one form of communication to another, with varying degrees of disruption and cohabitation by the technologies. In roughly the past 200 years, such disruptive "new media" have ranged from pamphleteering and penny presses to the telegraph and television; in every instance, the technology or techniques that challenged established media were a reflection of their circumstances as much as their revolutionary power. As Nicholas Lemann, dean of the Columbia Graduate School of Journalism, wrote in a *New Yorker* critique of internet journalism: "Societies create structures of authority for producing and distributing knowledge, information, and opinion. These structures are always waxing and waning, depending not only on the invention of new means of communication but also on political, cultural, and economic developments."

Citizen journalism, then, is as much a product of the technology as it of our times—our emphasis on individual empowerment and public transparency, not to mention our willingness to leave, quite publicly, bread crumbs of our personal life on social networking sites and in Google searches. We're increasingly out there, exposed online ... and finding that we're OK with that. Participatory culture plays into and reinforces this ethos of openness and publicness. All are invited to take part—on whatever level: posting photos to Flickr, creating fan blogs, or simply commenting on news stories—and equally share the benefits of having information more public and more immediate and more accessible than ever. And, yet, such a culture has developed in tandem with the technology. It's not just the internet itself, but the internet enhancements of the 21st century that have made participatory journalism possible. It's broadband-speed connections, almost universal now, that make video worth uploading and watching on YouTube. It's Web 2.0 software and sensibilities that encourage decentralized, networked, bottom-up creation and distribution of content. It's the low-cost barriers to entry afforded by Google's free stuff, ubiquitous camera phones, Twitter for distribution, and $150 Flip video recorders. No printing press, broadcast license or editor required. Just plug and play.

Of course, such grandiose descriptions tend to oversimplify the situation; even if potentially millions can contribute online, relatively few of them do in any major way, and perhaps fewer still enjoy their stay in today's "user-generated purgatory" of never-ending drivel. Nevertheless, web technologies have unleashed a citizen-participation force unlike anything seen in the history of media. We can only expect a broadening and deepening base of such communication tools in the future.

ENVISIONING WEB 3.0

From a technological perspective, will citizen journalism in 2025 look anything like it does in 2010? For that matter, what of the internet as a whole? While long-term prognostications are notoriously tricky—after all, the Mosaic web browser was launched barely 15 years ago, and only, um, a few things have changed since then—this much is clear: The current model for online journalism (both citizen and professional) is a *desktop* model. That is, it is best accomplished from a computer and displayed on conventional web pages. Indeed, this is true for all of Web 2.0; for all the revolutionary rhetoric it has inspired, the second-generation internet remains a desktop-oriented platform, whether you're talking about blogs, RSS feeds, wikis, photo-sharing, or social networking.

The future, by contrast, points to a *mobile* model. While handhelds and smartphones have been around for some time, the release of Apple's iPhone in 2007 heralded a new era, one in which the consumption *and* creation of multimedia could take place anywhere, anytime. In this next phase, perhaps a Web 3.0 for media generally, citizen journalism becomes a truly mobile experience, giving new meaning to being "live" and "on the scene." We're already familiar with the impact of having camera phones in the hands of millions of people, particularly after the London subway bombings in 2005. But fast-forward to a video future and consider the likes of Qik.com. The fledgling site makes possible the "human satellite truck," as Jeff Jarvis calls it—the ability to broadcast live on the web from your video-equipped cell phone. "No big camera. No satellite uplink. No editing into packages. No b-roll. Just the news now." Such a scenario of live news creation makes YouTube, with its tedious editing and uploading required, seem lumbering by comparison. Reuters has already tried this. After successfully outfitting its mobile journalism (or "mojo") unit with Nokia multimedia phones and Bluetooth keyboards, it is thinking of doing the same for its fleet of reporters—as well as giving phones to selected "citizen experts."

Mobile video is just one peek into a future citizen journalism filled with images. As connectivity speeds increase and camera quality and ubiquity grow, the web will become more visual, and more visceral—more raw footage, less scripted reporting, more as-it-happens awareness shared by producer and audience alike. In such a world, participatory journalism will be less about words and blog posts as it will be about presenting one's audio-visual reality, in real-time, on the off-chance something of interest will occur. It will be livecasting, and *life*-casting. Indeed, both.

Even as blog posts become shorter and less about words, it's quite likely that their frequency will increase, created more fluidly from a mobile—rather than desktop—platform. Just witness the buzz over Twitter, which has taken mobile blogging (or, "moblogging") to new levels with its easy-to-send, easy-to-share *tweets*: messages of 140 characters designed to fit the dimensions of a cell phone text message. When other means failed, Twitter allowed a TV station to cover the runaway wildfires in San Diego, and later it carried the first reports of a massive earthquake in China. It's easy to imagine such phone-and-PC linking tools permeating the participatory journalism of the future, just as similar "push" technologies—synchronizing personal data and media files across multiple platforms—go mainstream with latest-generation iPhone software.

But if enhanced mobility marks the individual-citizen contribution to come, *crowdsourcing* unlocks the wisdom of the collective, and appears poised to become a key component of next-generation Citizen Journalism. Think of it as Wikipedia for journalism. Or, as Robert Niles of the Online Journalism Review defines it:

> Crowdsourcing, in journalism, is the use of a large group of readers to report a news story. It differs from traditional reporting in that the information collected is gathered not manually, by a reporter or team of reporters, but through some automated agent, such as a website. Stripped to its core, though, it's still just another way of reporting,

one that will stand along the traditional 'big three' of interviews, observation and examining documents.

Crowdsourcing fits neatly into a main tenet of citizen journalism: that professional reporters are not the exclusive arbiters of knowledge on a given subject; "the audience knows more collectively than the reporter alone," Glaser wrote. As a journalism method, crowdsourcing already has been used by some Big Media outlets, most notably when *The Dallas Morning News* asked readers to help it sort through a mountain of digitized records on the JFK assassination. But crowdsourcing is more naturally deployed by journalism upstarts with small staffs (e.g., Joshua Micah Marshall's Talking Points Memo) or those with virtually no staff at all (e.g., Jay Rosen's NewAssignment.net). In his review of crowdsourced journalism, Niles concludes with this prediction about its place in the future of citizen journalism:

> Unlike more traditional notions of "citizen journalism," crowdsourcing does not ask readers to become anything more than what they've always been: eyewitnesses to their daily lives. They need not learn advanced reporting skills, journalism ethics or how to be a better writer. It doesn't ask readers to commit hours of their lives in work for a publisher with little or no financial compensation. Nor does it allow any one reader's work to stand its own, without the context of many additional points of view. For those reasons, I think, crowdsourcing ultimately will revolutionize journalism as "citizen journalism" efforts that rely on more traditional reporting methods fail.

MOMENTUM: CONVERGENCE, CONCENTRATION, CONVERSATION

By 2007 and 2008, even as talk of citizen journalism had reached a fever pitch, questions were emerging about its long-term sustainability. The Bayosphere.com citizen journalism venture started by Dan Gillmor, the founding father, had already failed. Then the much-acclaimed Backfence.com, often cited in academic and industry articles as the shining example of citizen journalism, called it quits. Then, later that year, Steve Outing, who perhaps knew a successful model better than anyone after writing his seminal "11 Layers of Citizen Journalism" essay for the Poynter Institute, saw his own citizen-based venture flame out. Not enough professional content, he realized too late; plus, "you need to filter out and highlight the best user content, while downplaying the visibility of the mediocre stuff."

Was citizen journalism already waning, dying of neglect amid media abundance, or merely struggling to "monetize" itself in the short term? Perhaps these thoughts were on the mind of Oh Yeon-ho, founder and CEO of OhmyNews in South Korea. He opened his company's 2007 International Citizen Reporters' Forum with a cautionary tone: "[With more access to broadband internet worldwide,] the question looming large is increasingly less about 'digital opportunity' and more about how we can best manage the abundance of content, web platforms and user participation. While we are seeing an explosion of blogs, an equal number of bloggers are leaving cyberspace at the same time out of frustration at the scarcity of response. After all, how many bloggers do you remember?"

Around the same time, a team of researchers began a study called Tracking and Analyzing Community News Models. They conducted an audit of the 64 citizen journalism sites they found in 15 U.S. metro areas. One surprising, and particularly troubling, finding emerged: Despite the talk of transparency and interactivity, most of the citizen media sites analyzed were more tightly controlled by gatekeepers than professional news sites; only 27% allowed users to upload content to the site. Such insularity might be expected of fledgling websites, most staffed by volunteers only, but the findings underscore a larger point about citizen journalism: It's very much under construction.

That uncertainty makes predicting its future path all the more challenging. Yet, prevailing trends in participatory culture point to an increasingly empowered audience, one able to create, critique, and collaborate content more seamlessly than ever before. Thus, despite the mixed record so far, there's momentum for citizen journalism. There are driving forces of pro-am convergence, of audience fragmentation and concentration, and of hunger for conversation that are setting the stage for the future of collaborative journalism—online, offline, and perhaps in the mobile spaces in between.

CONVERGENCE

In the 1990s, media convergence often meant local newspapers partnering with local television stations, amid a wider push throughout media for consolidation and conglomeration. Today, convergence in journalism is an effort to connect the newsroom with the outside world. If the first phase of convergence was about cutting costs and expanding coverage, the second is about mere survival.

But convergence isn't simply an organizational reshuffling. As we discussed earlier, it's a culture, an ethic, a revised way of thinking about media production and consumption. And, in journalism generally and participatory journalism in particular, it's upending not only long-standing structures and norms but also reconfiguring relationships among journalists, sources, and audience in unpredictable ways—creating a mash-up, if you will. A convergence of news platforms, roles, and styles will dominate the citizen journalism of the future.

Let's begin with the coming convergence of platforms. For the newspaper industry, the convergence of print and online models seems inevitable, with the latter finally eclipsing the former in total advertising revenue (and thus organizational emphasis) sometime around 2020 or beyond, depending on whom you ask. Given that participatory journalism occurs more easily online than in print, this shift is certain to lend more prominence and possibility to user-generated content—enabling, for example, more distributed, wisdom-of-the-crowd kind of reporting. This transition will alter gatekeeping, too. As news organizations cut staff and retrench their resources, we could see a move from user-generated creation to user-generated control. This is already occurring with the likes of CNN's iReport, which announced itself this way:

> What if we turned this site over to you? What if we allowed people to post raw video and tell stories you'd never see on CNN? What if it had politically incorrect speech?

What if it didn't matter if the stories were balanced? What if, instead of us confirming every nuance, we trusted you to determine what was and what wasn't accurate?

What if we created a site where the community—not CNN—became the "Most Trusted Name in News"?

And so, we developed iReport.com. Don't kid yourselves. This content is not pre-vetted or pre-read by CNN. This is your platform. In some journalistic circles, this is considered disruptive, even controversial! But we know the news universe is changing. We know that even here, at CNN, we can't be everywhere, all the time following all the stories you care about. So, we give you iReport.com. You will program it, you will police it; you will decide what's important, what's interesting, what's news.

Not coincidentally, CNN keeps its distance from the unwashed masses using its citizen-reporting venture, with nary a link to CNN.com on the iReport home page. This tension in convergence, of providing platforms for user engagement on the one hand while maintaining brand purity on the other, is occurring even within non-mainstream news sites that increasingly must navigate the professional-amateur dichotomy. Take, for instance, the Huffington Post. It has what co-founder Jonah Peretti calls the "mullet strategy." (Put another way, on Peretti's BuzzFeed site: "Business up front, party in the back.") In an interview with the *New Yorker*, Peretti said: "User-generated content is all the rage, but most of it totally sucks." The mullet strategy encourages readers to "argue and vent on the secondary pages, but professional editors keep the front page looking sharp. The mullet strategy is here to stay, because the best way for web companies to increase traffic is to let users have control, but the best way to sell advertising is a slick, pretty front page where corporate sponsors can admire their brands." For the Huffington Post's editorial process, this means front-page material gets edited while off-the-front blog posts get checked after they're posted—and then only if there are egregious problems. Thus, as convergence blurs traditional distinctions between professional and amateur, as new platforms emerge and journalistic roles converge, we can envision a hybrid journalism of the future: Some professional oversight for the up-front news; some collective, blogging-style quality control on the back end; and increased transparency and trust built into everything in between. It won't be perfect, of course, and a lot of good public affairs reporting will be lost in the process. Moreover, many newspapers and other new news ventures will never reach the critical mass to survive online, or in whatever other media format comes next. But, amid the creative destruction of 20th century news models, there's sufficient opportunity for experimentation with pro-am journalism to warrant some optimism for the future of converged journalism.

CONCENTRATION

Even as news media seek to expand their horizontal reach through convergence, linking with media allies and an active audience, their content will become more vertical in scope—not so much hyperlocal as hyper*narrow*, dedicated to an increasingly niche area of interest. This is the Long Tail brought to new(s) media economics. As fewer and fewer journalism outlets have the resources to cover general news for a general audience—and make any money doing it—audiences for news, like audiences for other media, will move from being broad and shallow to narrow and deep. A number of news startups, many of them funded by nonprofits or the Knight News Challenge contest, have taken this route, providing intensely localized coverage of communities, often in places where investigative reporting has slackened—such as with Voice of San Diego and MinnPost.com. While both of those sites feature professionally produced content, both reflect a more open-door approach that means greater engagement with local citizens and experts.

Perhaps this trend reflects not so much a desire for geographically localized information as much as uniquely *personal* news—news about the 150 people I know best, or information about whether my train is on time, or word on whether my neighbor's house sold (and at what price). This idea, of the hyper-personal trumping the hyper-local, began coalescing in 2008, as advocates of participatory journalism started debating: Do most people really care about local news? (Or, as Amy Gahran nicely put it in her Poynter blog post on the subject: "What if we are Wii bowling alone—and like it?") In the discussion that followed, Steve Outing offered this trenchant observation:

> 'Dog bites man' is newsworthy if you know the man, or dog, so nicely sums up what I've been thinking for some time about what many have termed "hyper-local" journalism.
>
> I've been saying for some time that sites like the defunct Backfence.com and (still-running) Yourhub.com contain boring content. That is, boring to everyone but a select few who know the kid who hit the game-winning home run, or the woman who won the local Volunteer of the Year award, or the guy who got bit by a dog.
>
> I *do* care if a guy a couple streets over in my neighborhood crashed his car or got arrested for indecent exposure; perhaps I know him, or pass him when walking the dog. I couldn't care less about the guy who lives in a neighborhood across town and won an award or got arrested for drunk driving.
>
> Deliver me hyper-personal news, not hyper-local. This really gets back to the old Daily Me concept. But now we have the technology to make that happen, and a growing well of this micro-local news from which to tap (local bloggers, websites of various local organizations, social network pages by local people, etc.—as well as from the newspaper staff's reporting, of course).

In other words, as Outing and others have explained, "dog bites man" is newsworthy if you know the man … or the dog. The essence is in delivering Daily Me of news and information that speaks to specialized, person-by-person interests. "To critics of hyper-local news or 'citizen journalism,'" Outing wrote, "I will argue that it can be powerful stuff when and only when it's targeted well. I can envision a future—and I look forward to it—when services are available to send me news on my smartphone letting me know that the guy down the street got bit by a dog." Which would be interesting to know—especially if it's your dog.

CONVERSATION

As the audience fragments into ever-narrow niches, what implications will that have for the quality of conversation that is so prized by citizen journalism ventures? One of the problems of our (post)modern existence is the increasing insularity of our suburban lives, cocooned as they are within a bubble of technology—cell phones as we drive, iPods as we jog, and social networking that keeps us plugged in at home rather than, well, socializing. Who talks to their neighbors anymore? Enter the likes of Front Porch Forum, a site that is both concentrated and conversation-oriented. It offers e-mail forums limited exclusively to physical neighborhoods in Chittenden County, Vermont. As Mark Glaser writes in his profile of the site: "Rather than being free-wheeling, anything-goes forums, FPF has been able to build more civil discussions by having people include their full name, street name and email address with each post. And users rave about how the site helps them connect with neighbors, find a lost pet or a good landlord, and even complain directly to local government officials."

Such civility is a silver lining for a future of fragmented media, but it raises a question posed by critics of participatory news: "The content of most citizen journalism will be familiar to anybody who has ever read a church or community newsletter—it's heartwarming and it probably adds to the store of good things in the world, but it does not mount the collective challenge to power which the traditional media are supposedly too timid to take up," as Nicholas Lemann wrote in the *New Yorker*. Yet, such critiques often miss the point: Participatory news is not *the* future of professional reporting, nor the destruction of it. It is not a utopian vision of citizen involvement, nor is it a dystopian picture of user-generated-content purgatory. Rather, it is an add-on, a hybrid, a mash-up. It will support, rather than supplant, the future of professional journalism, and could make it stronger yet as journalists teach and train and citizens engage and inform—working together to build trust, transparency, and depth of knowledge about communities and the people in them.

CONFRONTING ETHICS IN THE FUTURE

To close, let's return to Mayhill Fowler, the 61-year-old citizen reporter for the Huffington Post. Two months after she became famous for reporting on Obama's "bitter" comment, Fowler was in South Dakota on the final day of the grueling primary season. It was a Bill Clinton rally, and the former president was moving along the rope line, pressing palms with the crowd and fielding well wishes from all sides. Amid the crush and confusion and cell phone cameras, Fowler reached toward the former president. She wanted to ask for an interview with his wife but somehow dropped her business card just as she clasped Clinton's hand. Hastily, she blurted above the din: "Mister President, what do you think about that hatchet job somebody did on you in *Vanity Fair* … ?" Unaware of Fowler's media status or the digital recorder in her free hand, Clinton unloaded, calling the article's author "slimy," "sleazy" and a "scumbag," as well as turning his anger on other topics for several minutes.

Fowler's blog post on the exchange, including the damning audio evidence, again set off instant controversy, and played into the media narrative that Bill Clinton had become unhinged in the final hours of his wife's campaign. But among journalists, a different debate emerged, circulating around a nagging question: Why didn't Fowler ever identify herself? Moreover, why did she ask the question so provocatively? Those concerns troubled even Jay Rosen, co-founder of OffTheBus.net, and he acknowledged a lack of guidelines for such situations—but, then, who would have imagined a citizen journalist capturing two of the most incendiary quotes of the campaign season?

It's important not to make too much of the Fowler case—as with Obama, the Clinton quote flared for a few days but quickly fell off the media radar—but it serves to remind us that the ethics of participatory news are a work in progress, like the form of journalism itself. This is new territory. On the one hand, it's good for democracy if politicians have a harder time concealing their true selves … and yet, on the other hand, candidates' heightened awareness of always-on recorders and baiting citizen journalists is likely to make their appearances and comments more banal than ever, as one Poynter Institute ethics expert noted. More broadly, at the intersection of ethics and professionalism, journalists (with their norms of objectivity and detachment) and citizens (with their for-all-to-see passions and partisanship) must learn to negotiate for the public's trust on their own terms, whether in a competing or complementary way. "Neutrality is one way of being trusted, transparency another," Rosen wrote. "When we admit the validity of both, we expand the social space of the press. That is a good thing. If it has pro and amateur wings maybe the press can fly again."

SUGGESTED READING

Allan, Stuart, and Thorsen, Einar (2009). *Citizen Journalism: Global Perspectives.* New York: Peter Lang.

Beckett, Charlie (2008). *SuperMedia: Saving Journalism So It Can Save the World.* London: Blackwell.

Bruns, Axel (2008). *Blogs, Wikipedia, Second Life, and Beyond: From Production to Produsage.* New York: Peter Lang.

Gillmor, Dan (2004). *We the Media: Grassroots Journalism by the People, for the People.* Sebastopol, CA: O'Reilly Media.

Also, please refer to two key issues of *Nieman Reports*: "Is Local News the Answer?" (Vol. 61, No. 4, Winter 2007) and "Citizen Journalism" (Vol. 59, No. 4, Winter 2005).

Chapter 6

Cutbacks, Countermeasures and Consequences

Brian Baresch

"Reporters are faced with the daily choice of painstakingly researching stories or writing whatever people tell them. Both approaches pay the same."
—Scott Adams, *The Dilbert Principle*

IN THE LONG RUN, the legacy news organizations as well as new-media newcomers will work out sustainable business models or go down trying. In the long run, newspapers, TV news and online news sites will work out effective ways to engage the needs of their readers and viewers. In the long run, the questions raised in earlier chapters will get some answers.

But we don't get the news in the long run. We get the news every day, every minute if we want. A successful news setup six years in the future won't help us make sense of the economy or national security today, or explain the candidates and propositions by Election Day, or alert us to government and business actions that affect us. The future isn't here yet; legacy media are still doing the lion's share of the news reporting in the United States. As we wait for the inevitable shakeout, those struggling media companies have to make do with less while they put out the daily news. As newspapers, especially, send reporters and editors packing, those who remain have a larger workload to shoulder, and they face a growing cadre of official spokespeople and public-relations workers whose job it is to get their employers' views past the gatekeepers and into the paper. It comes as no surprise that the news staffs often find themselves overmatched and that even the hardest-working reporter has less time to check facts and filter her sources before the presses run.

The overworked reporter won't be getting much help in the foreseeable future, so she and her editors must change their approach to newsgathering. Some innovative approaches to the product and the mission are showing signs of success. News organizations may ultimately succeed with a sweeping redefinition of the public service they provide.

WHY TRY TO DO MORE WITH LESS?

The slide in readership and viewership is most pronounced among daily newspapers, so this chapter will focus on them, although the principles apply to other media as well. Newspaper circulation nationwide has been declining since the mid-1990s (in fact, the papers have been losing market share since the 1950s), gradually at first and then precipitously since 2004.

Newsroom employment peaked in 2001, at the crest of the tech bubble, according to the American Society of Newspaper Editors' annual newsroom census; since then, many papers have reduced their reporting and editing numbers through attrition, buyouts and layoffs. Consider the San Jose (Calif.) Mercury-News, which had 175 people working in its newsroom as of March 2008, down from 400 in 2001; in September 2009 the newsroom's online contact list had 120 names, encompassing reporters, photographers, assigning editors and support staff (but not copy editors).

Overall, the job losses, like circulation losses, have intensified in recent years. When 2,000 newspaper jobs (in and out of the newsroom) were lost in 2005, *Editor & Publisher* called it the top industry story of the year. But that was small potatoes compared with 2008, when newsrooms alone suffered 5,900 job cuts, according to the American Society of News Editors. The carnage prompted *Editor & Publisher* to conclude at the end of 2008: "Somehow, newspaper owners continue to think that the way to handle economic downturns is to make their product worse be eliminating its most important asset, people. But with fewer reporters to dig up news as newspapers transition to the web their content is going to look more and more like everything else online, limited and poorly reported." That wasn't the end, either. In September 2009, UNITY: Journalists of Color, a coalition of trade groups, examined news organizations' self-reporting and SEC filings and reported that the news industry had shed 35,000 jobs in the previous 12 months. (That figure includes non-newsroom categories such as circulation and advertising, so it is difficult to make direct comparisons with other studies.) Layoffs continued in 2009 at well over 1,000 per month, sometimes more than 2,000.

Why would a struggling industry release its key quality workers? Philip Meyer, in *The Vanishing Newspaper*, supplies one possible answer. Meyer lines up evidence that increasing the quality of journalism leads to increased profit for the newspaper's owners, as readers come to trust its reporting and depend on it for information. However, the relationship is not linear; eventually, as quality improves (presumably through the hiring and support of more good journalists), profits will level off and even start declining; this is the law of diminishing returns. The point where profits level off is the "sweet spot," Meyer says, and if a newspaper is beyond the sweet spot, it can reduce its newsroom staffing and actually increase its profitability.

However, finding the sweet spot is harder than it sounds; trust and the resultant profit from increased quality take time to build up, but the cost is immediate. If a newspaper assumes it is past the point of diminishing returns and can afford to let people go, it will become more profitable if it is correct but will lose if it is wrong.

An extreme example, cited by Meyer, was that of the Thomson Newspapers, which were the subject of a 1998 case study by Stephen Lacy and Hugh J. Martin. The Thomson chain during the 1980s combined price increases and cost cuts to achieve high profit margins, in the process gaining a reputation for poor journalism; however, by 1990 the chain had lost circulation and its profits dropped, while across the country non-Thomson newspapers of similar size were actually gaining circulation.

'CHURNALISM'

In 2007 a group at the University of Cardiff, Wales, undertook some empirical research into the effects of newsroom staffing changes. The researchers studied five British national daily newspapers: the *Times*, the *Guardian*, the *Independent*, and the *Daily Telegraph* (all considered "quality" papers) and the mid-market *Daily Mail*. They examined two weeks of each publication, a total of 2,207 domestic stories, to establish the extent to which each depended upon public-relations information, wire-service copy or other media material. The study was commissioned by journalist Nick Davies for his 2008 book *Flat Earth News*. The circumstances of Fleet Street are unique to Britain, as we will see, but results of staff cuts can serve as a caution for U.S. news organizations.

Fully 60 percent of the stories consisted entirely or mostly of wire copy (mainly from the Press Association, roughly equivalent to the Associated Press in the United States), PR material, or both. An additional 20 percent contained noticeable amounts of wire or PR copy along with local reporting. In 8 percent of stories the source was unclear. That left a mere 12 percent of stories across the five newspapers in which all the material was clearly generated by the reporters themselves.

This was not apparent to the casual reader of these Fleet Street newspapers. In a practice that would cause scandals in the United States, only one in 100 stories was identified as coming from the wire service; most carried a byline attributing the story to "a staff reporter" or even to a named reporter who had apparently simply rewritten the PA wire copy. Public-relations copy was similarly disguised.

The Cardiff researchers also found that in the relatively few stories that were based on specific factual claims, a full 70 percent of those claims went into print completely uncorroborated; in only 12 percent of those stories did the reporter fully investigate the central claim. "Taken together," the researchers concluded, "these data portray a picture of the journalistic processes of news gathering and news reporting in which any meaningful independent journalistic activity by the press is the exception rather than the rule. We are not talking about investigative journalism here, but the everyday practices of news judgement, fact checking, balance, criticising and interrogating sources etc., that are, in theory, central to routine, day-to-day journalism practice."

How is it that "routine, day-to-day journalism practice" has become anything but routine in Britain's most highly regarded newspapers? The researchers also examined newsroom staffing levels and the news holes in the Fleet Street papers, where squeezing money through staff cuts has been the norm for years. It turns out that staffing is roughly the same as it was in 1985, but each reporter is responsible now for three times as much copy. Essentially, each inch of copy produced by each reporter must be generated in one-third the time that was allowed two decades ago. Davies calls the result "churnalism."

A similar scenario comes from Chris Ayres in *War Reporting for Cowards*. He described being sent to New York as the Wall Street correspondent for the *Times* of London, expecting a life of power lunches and mergers and acquisitions. What he found instead, being essentially a one-person bureau, was "lift and view"—lift ideas from the *New York Times* and view cable news for information. "I had expected something more glamorous," he wrote. "Given the number of stories I had to write, and the wide range of subjects to cover, it was almost impossible to make insider 'contacts'—the PRs, bankers, and analysts who usually supply journalists with scoops."

Meanwhile, the BBC's television news division was doing its own cost cutting, with similar effects on the finished product. Davies writes that some provincial TV reporters were handed video cameras and told to shoot and edit their own visuals as do-it-all video journalists, which left them less time for fact-checking. Some former cameramen and editors were cross-trained as reporters and turned into VJs as well.

Even newspaper stories that rely mainly or solely on wire copy are not free of public-relations influence, because wire reporters are under the same constraints as newspaper employees, and receive the same pressure from public-relations workers. So in the case of wire stories, the PR influence often is there as well, simply one step removed.

Britain's press has reached this state of affairs after two full decades of cost-cutting wars; Davies dates the beginning of Fleet Street's decline to 1986, when Rupert Murdoch broke the unions at the newspapers he owned and immediately set about looking to cut costs and increase profits; the competing newspapers had to follow suit. The newspaper industry in the United States has seen cost-cutting in the same time frame but, until recently, nothing nearly so drastic.

Reporters in the United States may find themselves under more and more pressure, however. The Bureau of Labor Statistics of the U.S. Department of Labor projects that nationwide employment of news analysts, reporters and correspondents, which includes both broadcast and print journalists, will increase 2 percent from 2006 to 2016, from about 67,000 to 68,000. In the same period, public-relations specialists are expected to increase their numbers by 18 percent, from 243,000 to 286,000. Those numbers obviously must be treated as gross estimates, since the continuing rapid pace of technological change makes any projection murky. But the expected trends do not bode well for independent journalism.

A larger concern in an environment where PR workers far outnumber the journalists too busy to filter their work is that the public-relations industry may be setting the agenda for the public by default. The Cardiff study's authors reported that "at least 41 percent of press articles and 52 percent of broadcast news items contain PR materials which play an agenda-setting role or where PR material makes up the bulk of the story." It is widely recognized that the news media, by selecting and emphasizing certain stories over others, play a role in determining what topics citizens think about, and some research indicates that news stories affect readers' opinions about the issues beyond simply providing them with information to consider.

The Cardiff study shows what can happen when the normal balance between sources and reporters is heavily skewed in favor of outside pressure as publicists grow in number and journalists' power to choose the time they devote to each story declines. As public-relations officers provide more of the story ideas, perspectives and information on which the news is based, both directly to news outlets and through wire services, the universe of ideas and points of view will shrink. "The immediate impact of this is to create a consensus account of the world, in which most of the outlets draw most of their stories and angles and quotes from a tiny collection of raw material," Davies writes.

JUST BECAUSE IT'S IN THE PAPER …

A rigorous study like the one done by the Cardiff team has not been essayed for the news media in the United States. In the U.S. tradition, practices such as passing along wire copy or news releases as staff-written stories are strongly discouraged, and reporters seemingly have more time for interviews, research and fact-checking than the "churnalists" toiling on Fleet Street. But the influence of publicists, there and elsewhere, is impossible to avoid.

Indeed, "Unpaid placement masquerading as actual article"—PR posing as news—is one facet of a less rigorous but useful critique of U.S. news media that takes the form of a news-aggregating website, Fark.com. The site's proprietor, Drew Curtis, posts links to oddball news items with snarky comments attached. As Curtis describes it in *It's Not News, It's Fark: How Mass Media Tries to Pass Off Crap As News*, as he was reading more than 1,000 stories a day to find material for the site, he began noticing patterns of "Not News" articles seemingly written just to fill space. Besides product placement, they include fearmongering (hyping unlikely scenarios to create drama) and "Equal time for nutjobs," in which fringe characters are introduced to a story for the sake of providing the "other side" of a story that doesn't have another side.

A look at Fark.com during the writing of this chapter found an environmental health researcher's presentation on possible fungal infections in crops as a result of global warning that became a story of impending "killer cornflakes;" a major network news in-depth report on large-breasted women who get breast reductions to alleviate back pain; and the outgoing president's daughter's wedding getting saturation coverage in the news media despite having no reporters present—every photo and description on TV and in the paper came straight from the president's publicists.

WHERE WE ARE

The Project for Excellence in Journalism's 2008 State of the Media report describes the in-between nature of U.S. news media as the past fades away and the future seems no closer than before. As noted before, there are fewer and fewer journalists working harder and harder to produce the news we rely on; meanwhile, the vision of a fully democratic online news environment with plenty of news sources and "niche" outlets remains elusive. The top 10 news websites mostly belong to legacy companies such as the *New York Times* and CNN, and they command a larger share of the audience—29 percent, according to Matthew Hindman's 2007 paper *Political Accountability and the Web's 'Missing Middle'*—than the top 10 newspapers' 19 percent. Blogs and public affairs websites are still relatively small in terms of audience, the PEJ report states, and their proprietors are not "average people," having more elite educations and post-graduate degrees than the top op-ed columnists. But as readers head to the legacy media's online sites, advertising dollars are not following: "The crisis in journalism, in other words, may not strictly be loss of audience. It may, more fundamentally, be the decoupling of news and advertising."

So as fewer people are asked to do more, the report states, the emphasis shifts from original reporting toward processing information—on its face, a move toward the Fleet Street model discussed earlier. But the PEJ report suggests that this is not a degradation of the reporting job so much as a component of a paradigm shift that is still in progress. News is becoming less of a product and more of a service: The readers don't just want the events of the day; they want to be able to use the information. (More on this below.)

If the paradigm is shifting, then all the news business's assumptions are put into play. The legacy news organizations have operated for decades under the model of professional journalists gathering information about society and its structures so that their readers can make the informed choices in the voting booth and elsewhere that are required for democracy and civil society to function. Get into a discussion with reporters or, especially, editors about the role of the journalist in modern society and the words "sacred trust" will usually come up. The professional model, with standardization and essentially interchangeable journalists from one newsroom to the next, has been the standard for long enough that most of us can hardly envision journalism in any other way. But the professional era is in fact a historical anomaly; entrepreneurial journalism, without large national chains, held sway from the late 18th century well into the 20th. And the professional era isn't going away quietly; many of its practitioners have published broadsides against the new forms of information flow, especially blogs, the unregulated, often messy journals that anyone can produce. Without professional standards and professional editing, goes the argument, we can't trust anything in these new media.

But as the legacy media continue to reduce staff through layoffs, buyouts and attrition, some inside and outside journalism are asking whether those professional standards are a necessity or a luxury. The standards of journalism are largely upheld and enforced by a cadre of editors at each news organization; Alan Mutter, a former newspaper editor, current businessman and frequent blogger ("Reflections of a Newsosaur"), got a discussion going in February 2008 when he raised the question of whether newspapers could afford all those editors. How many times should a story be read before it gets committed to print or the web?

At the typical metro daily, five or more editors may handle a story before it goes to press. Blogs are normally one-person operations; group blogs have multiple contributors, but they don't typically edit one another's posts. And the news aggregator Google News gathers and presents information without human intervention at all. Since, as we saw in the Cardiff study, the news hole can be filled with a skeleton staff and low standards, the temptation to reduce headcount is strong. As Mutter concluded: "While there is no doubt about the value of the industry's traditional values, the question is whether the industry can continue to afford them."

The writer Nicholas Carr expressed a similar sentiment at Brittanica.com:

Speaking before the Online Publishing Association in 2006, the head of the *New York Times'* web operation, Martin Nisenholtz, summed up the dilemma facing newspapers today. He asked the audience a simple question: "How do we create high-quality content in a world where advertisers want to pay by the click, and consumers don't want to pay at all?"

The answer may turn out to be equally simple: We don't.

HOW IMPORTANT IS IMPORTANCE?

Mutter and Carr made harsh but realistic assessments of the position where the legacy news media find themselves. The question of how to pay for good journalism is a stubborn one. New York University journalism professor and PressThink blogger Jay Rosen explicitly agrees with Carr:

> I think he's right. It's possible we will lose some of the public goods that newspapers under the old [advertising] subsidy system were able to bring forward. People ask me about this all the time. When I tell them there's no answer at the moment a strange look comes across their faces. A social problem with no answer? Is that even allowed?

Of course the historically accurate fact that there's no answer makes it an exciting moment in news. The fact that we could lose something makes it somewhat urgent. The "sacred trust" school of journalism is worried, and rightly so. But it may be that losing some of the vital public goods will be good for journalism.

As Michael Hirschorn wrote in the *Atlantic*, much of journalism in the past 50 years has been reporting on the Important events around the world—Russian politics, Congressional debates, City Council meetings, the stories that any Educated Person should know about. Readers who wanted or needed information had few ways to get it—the daily paper, a weekly newsmagazine, the evening news. So the news didn't have to be very interesting to draw an audience.

But the "Be the Broccoli" model was leaky; it slowly lost market share, as circulation gains did not keep up with population increases. Now that much of the "hard news"—the stuff that previously would have appeared almost exclusively on front pages of newspapers—is widely available anywhere and anytime in the digital environment, providing important news is not sufficient. Indeed, now that a large part of the national and global news report is essentially a commodity, putting it in the paper is most likely not even necessary.

Hirschorn proposed "a radical notion:" "Stop being important and start being interesting." He even proposed a convenient way to measure "interesting" in terms of readers: the "most popular" lists of stories that every news site puts on its front page. His comparison of the roster of most e-mailed stories with those on the front page of the print edition of three large newspapers surprised him:

> I had expected the most–e-mailed results to track the lineups of the more baldly audience-focused TV newscasts, which have increasingly made a fetish of "news that matters to you," and hence are packed with tedious features on your health, your real estate, your job, your children, and so forth. Instead, the most–e-mailed lists, despite a smattering of parochial concerns, were a rich stew of global affairs, provocative insight, hot-button issues, pop culture, compelling narrative, and enlightened localism. In short, they were interesting. What they were not, generally, was important, at least not in the grand tectonic geopolitical sense.

The top e-mailed stories overlapped with the editors' choices for the front page less than one time in four. Hirschorn said the results suggest "that readers might no longer need newspapers for news. And by 'news' I mean the traditional newspaper functions of reporting on congressional hearings, city-council meetings, sporting events, earnings reports, and so forth." Those stories are available in many places. The stories on the e-mailed list, on the other hand, were each unique—the "Hey, Mabel" stories beloved of editors everywhere. "These stories, as they say in marketing, offer a 'value add,' something that's not available on the vaguely Soviet-seeming syndication-fed news pages of AOL, Yahoo, or Google. The real value now lies in non-commodifiable virtues like deep reporting, strong narrative, distinct point of view, and sharp analysis." A re-imagined front page would [do] away with the soggy middle of commodity news in favor of a high-low mix of agenda-setting reportage and analysis, strong storytelling on topics not being covered everywhere else, and saucy, knowing takeouts on people the readership actually cares about. It would, in essence, invert the traditional relationship the newspaper has with readers. The old front page assumed your interest; the new front page would earn it.

The PEJ State of the Media report noted a similar finding from its surveys. Citizens, it said, wanted more coverage of "bread-and-butter issues, such as rising gas prices, toy recalls, and the legislative battle over children's health insurance," and less of news such as certain aspects of the debate over the Iraq war or the crisis in Pakistan and other events from far away.

These findings suggest a strategy that the CUNY journalism professor and Buzz Machine blogger Jeff Jarvis calls "Cover what you do best; link to the rest." Space in the print editions is declining—the print editions themselves are even shrinking in some cases, as companies conserve paper by using a narrower web—and the editorial real estate is too valuable for commodity information. Newspapers can put "value-add" stories and features into the print edition and provide commodity news (or links to it) on their web pages. As Jarvis writes: "We no longer need to be all things to all people. We can link to niche coverage that is better than what we could have afforded to offer ourselves. We also no longer need to waste resources on ego, on all having our own television critics or golf columnists, on sending one-too-many reporters to the big story that is all over TV just so we can say we have our byline there."

That will be easier said than done. Many newsrooms are conservative organizations resistant to change and innovation, still stuck in the sacred-trust, we-decide-what's-news model. At one virtual water cooler, Testy Copy Editors (www.testycopyeditors.org), veteran editors from various newsrooms mock new news efforts such as crowdsourcing or blogs. Linking outside the newspaper's own site is also problematic for some. Still, some are adapting.

Once the news model changes from "most important" to "most interesting," with links to commodity news, the news organization is free to focus on stories it can do better than anyone else, especially local news. At the same time it can seek the best source to link to for coverage of any topic. Jarvis uses the I. Lewis "Scooter" Libby trial in early 2007 as an example. Libby, a former top aide to Vice President Dick Cheney, was tried on obstruction of justice and perjury charges. A group blog, Firedoglake, live-blogged the trial with knowledgeable contributors, and both Jarvis and Jay Rosen called it the best source for keeping up with the proceedings. A news site aiming to provide up-to-the-minute coverage of the trial would have simply had to link to Firedoglake.com, then follow up later in the day with analysis from the wire services.

(It should be noted that linking outside the news site may seem unnatural to some wary news managers. They fear that linking to outside content, especially blogs, was dangerous because the paper would face a libel suit if the target site ever defamed anyone.)

Already strategies are emerging for using links to full advantage. One entrepreneur is Scott Karp, co-founder and chief executive of Publish2, which makes an aggregation platform for online news sites that helps dynamically organize and publish links to outside content. On his blog Publishing 2.0, Karp offered some examples: A Tennessee newspaper added to its coverage of a big basketball game by aggregating about a dozen blogs in the area that were commenting on the game. And a paper in Illinois supplemented its coverage of a school shooting with an aggregation of other coverage online. In each case the news site not only offered its own take on the news but also made itself the gateway to coverage across the web.

PUTTING IT INTO PRACTICE

So what does "most interesting" look like on the page? The blogger Josh Korr ("Korr Values") was for two years a news editor at tbt* (Tampa Bay Times), a free daily tabloid published by the *St. Petersburg Times*. As Korr describes it, tbt* started in 2004 as a weekly with mostly entertainment and lifestyle-type stories aimed at young readers; then in 2006 it went daily, expanding its original tone and approach to local and national news and sports, with consumer news, opinion pages, interesting photos (newsy or not) and an aggregation of interesting web content. The approach to news is to consider the effect of the events on the reader—most of the "traditional" newspaper lineup of national and world events and politics has no discernible effect on most readers, and most readers don't care about it. Korr said he follows continuing stories but waits to put, say, Washington political news into the paper until something interesting prompts a roundup of the story so far. This represents not an abandonment but a re-imagining of the newspaper's Fourth Estate role. tbt* now claims more than 370,000 readers per week.

Korr also addressed the challenge of making the print version of the news product as interesting as the hyperlinked web. He recommended taking a long view toward setting up some sort of rights or wire service that would allow the paper to put web content on paper. In the meantime, news editors can report on unique stories found online and print links to the original material. The key, for Korr, is to avoid predictability; if the reader doesn't know what she will find in today's paper, she is more likely to keep picking it up.

In Boston, an upstart free daily commuter paper called BostonNOW innovated with "reverse-publishing"—starting with a blogger corps online, then putting the best posts into the paper, along with original reporting from paid staffers. Within a year, BostonNOW's audited daily circulation reached 119,000 and it had plenty of large advertisers. But in mid-April 2008 its Icelandic owners, beset by catastrophic economic conditions in their home country, abruptly pulled the plug and shut the paper down.

Of course, it is impossible to say whether BostonNOW would have continued to grow and thrive if the Icelandic economy had not deteriorated as quickly as it did, or if the paper had had more solvent investors. But we must hope that someone tries it again. BostonNOW and tbt* are the rarest of 21st-century birds: new daily newspapers that started out strong. They did so by approaching the news from a reader's standpoint, putting the agenda-driven stories on a siding until they were needed and instead providing catchy, unpredictable journalism that drew readers in without pandering.

The mantra of doing more with less can lead to disaster or to innovation and unfamiliar territory. American journalism may follow the Fleet Street model and surrender a great deal of control to business and government PR agents; it can keep trying to do what it has been doing for decades; or it can take a fresh look at its mission and its audience to make the most of the resources it has left.

SUGGESTED READING

Davies, Nick. (2008). *Flat Earth News: An award-winning reporter exposes falsehood, distortion and propaganda in the global media.* London: Chatto & Windus.

Meyer, Philip. (2006). *The vanishing newspaper: Saving journalism in the information age.* Columbia, MO: University of Missouri Press.

Chapter 7

Two Other Views—
Infotainment and Alternative Press

Paul Alonso and Jaime Loke

IN JANUARY 2008, THE Los Angeles assistant bureau chief of the Associated Press (AP) told his staff in a memo: "Now and for the foreseeable future, virtually everything involving Britney [Spears] is a big deal." The memo encouraged reporters to work to confirm stories about the pop icon so they could make it to the wire. The memo was reproduced in blogs about journalism, and reanimated questioning of journalistic values. In fact, this was an illustrative example of journalistic codes in an era in which entertainment informs the news agenda and increasingly plays an essential role in news judgment

"Fake news" icon Jon Stewart simultaneously skewered mainstream news and the community organization ACORN in September 2009 on "The Daily Show with Jon Stewart"—not with satire, but with the actual news. Stewart ridiculed the young activists who shot hidden-camera video as they asked ACORN to fund an expansion of their make-believe prostitution business. But Stewart also ridiculed mainstream media for leaving it to amateur filmmakers to break the story that ended ACORN's federal funding. "You're telling me that two kids from the cast of 'High School Musical 3' can break this story with a video camera and their grandmother's chinchilla coat? And you got nothing?" The AP wants more Britney Spears while the satire wants more hard news. This is not your father's journalism.

Media theorist and critic Guy Debord wrote about "the society of spectacle" 40 years ago but today's most important events—like the 9/11 attacks or the wars in Afghanistan and Iraq—are largely defined by what becomes iconic imagery in their media coverage, and scandals, celebrities, paparazzi, talk shows, and reality shows have become the preferred genres for audiences.

These phenomena have consequences for journalism and democracy. In a commercial media environment focused on ratings and advertising revenues, infotainment threatens the public-service ethos of journalism, which is critical for fostering informed democratic practices among citizens. News coverage of Barack Obama's election and inauguration reflected this trend. While critics on the right shouted charges of a left-leaning media bias, it's possible there was another factor at play. Many newspapers found themselves rushing to print extra copies on Nov. 5, 2008, because people were grabbing up what they viewed as history captured in print the day after the historic election. Whether due to history or celebrity, the lesson for publishers was clear: Obama sells.

In times of globalization, concentration of media ownership increases this trend while investigative journalism and minority programming are scarce commodities in both public and commercial media. There is a façade of diversity that exists in mainstream news media today.

From 24-hour cable news networks to myriad online news sites, the number of news sources seems out of this world. However, under closer scrutiny, these seemingly diverse sources of mainstream media are merely offspring of a select few umbrella companies. A single company owns CBS, MTV, Showtime and Comedy Central. Its sole owner, media giant Viacom, accounts for 30 cable channels and a half-dozen film studios. This is the mystery behind why cable providers have to offer tiered services rather than a la carte selections of channels to individual subscribes as these media conglomerates demand carriage of all their channels in one package and contain competitor must-carry rules as well. (In other words, if a cable package offers Viacom/Nickelodeon, it must also offer Disney, which also owns ABC; and if a provider offers Disney, it must also offer Disney's ESPN and ABC Family channels.)

The abundance of news is creating an information overload, where many viewers, bombarded with visuals, are unable to differentiate between public information and corporate propaganda. As the news media become increasingly commercialized, the need to make it entertaining—the E-factor—has become a crucial priority for "news" content producers. They borrow and adapt characteristics from entertainment genres.

Entertainment programs like Thursday night's *Survivor* on CBS become prominent "news" stories on the network's Friday morning *Early Show*. The tendency has been to follow a tabloid approach: circulate trivia, blend fact with fiction, and, critics say, even distort the truth.

The blurring of lines is a two-way street. Comedy Central's *The Daily Show* became such a hit over the last decade that its "lead reporter" Stephen Colbert spun off a second news satire homage. Now *The Daily Show* and its "fake news" progeny are often cited by young adults as a primary information source. Alaska Gov. Sarah Palin wasn't enough to rescue the Republican presidential ticket, but she was a godsend for *Saturday Night Live*, which went from life support to its highest ratings in a decade thanks to impersonator Tina Fey. Palin herself dropped by *SNL* shortly before Election Day. And recall that Arnold Schwarzenegger announced his California gubernatorial bid on the *Tonight Show with Jay Leno*. The prime time *Jay Leno* show, which began in the fall of 2009, put actress Drew Barrymore, sportscaster Bob Costas and newsman Brian Williams on equal footing—actually, equal seating, each taking turns behind the wheel of an electric car, hoping for the "immortality" of having their names on the leader board at Leno's back-lot race track.

In today's infotainment society, entertainment and spectacle have entered into all domains of economy, politics, society, and everyday life. As Douglas Kellner shows in his 2003 book *Media Spectacle*, contemporary expression is infused with a culture of spectacle, in film, theater, fashion, art, architecture, popular music, eroticism, video and computer games, among others. And if ever there was a canvas ripe for spectacle it is the internet, helping generate multimedia and networked infotainment societies. In *News as Entertainment: The Rise of Global Infotainment*, Daya Thussu describes this phenomenon as "global infotainment," meaning "the globalization of a U.S.-style ratings-driven television journalism which, like the penny press, favors the privatized soft news—about celebrities, crime, corruption and violence—and presents it as a form of spectacle, at the expense of news about political, civic and public affairs." Media scholar Robert McChesney describes a milquetoast news product designed, more than anything else, to offend the least amount of people. Infotainment also provides possibilities to promote alternative values and interpretations about society.

TABLOID NEWS ISN'T NEW

The history of journalism shows that crime, celebrity and human-interest stories are more marketable than coverage of political or policy issues. News as entertainment has a long tradition, from the broadside ballad to the yellow and tabloid press, from cinema newsreels to television. In Britain, the emergence of the newspaper press in the eighteenth century was aimed at gentlemen and the merchant classes, while the masses were entertained by street literature. The "broadside ballad" offered cheap and cheerful verses about sensational news and entertaining topics on crudely printed sheets, appealing to the visual through its typography and crude illustrations. This street literature was taken to a new level in the United States, launched by the "penny press" in the 1830s. At the time, newspapers were available only by subscription and sold for six cents apiece; the new penny papers sold for one cent and could be had by the day on any street corner. It turned out that a good way to sell more daily papers was to include a high quota of salacious stories related to crime and punishment, preferably involving young women or famous men.

But penny press visionaries like James Gordon Bennett found other ways to sell papers, including non-partisan coverage, expanded community news and the first beat reporting. In many ways, papers like that era's *New York Daily Herald*, the *World* and the *Globe* were the pillars on which modern objective reporting was built. It also produced economic and entertainment reach that enhanced the media's influence on society and the masses, while inaugurating the cult of celebrity. The development of the popular press was also supported by the rise of the advertising industry in the United States. By the end of the 19th century, advertising had become a powerful element in making the U.S. the most consumer-oriented society of the world and the new type of journalism was good for business.

American broadcasting had a commercial focus from its inception: the U.S. Radio Act of 1927 defined radio broadcasting as a commercial enterprise funded by advertising. Television also followed this model. As the networks' revenues were based on audience ratings, infotainment became central. The 1950s marked the appearance of classic entertainment programming: game and talent shows, glamour and celebrity shows, such as *Miss America*, and in 1954, the celebrity talk show *The Tonight Show*, which is still on the air. At the same time, journalists like Edward R. Murrow became as well-known and as idolized as matinee stars like Clark Gable.

Western Europe, especially Britain with the BBC, used a not-for-profit, public broadcasting monopoly that served their purposes well—until competition came along. By the end of the Cold War in 1989, especially after the fall of the Berlin Wall, market capitalism overwhelmed the state-driven model of broadcasting, even in the Western nations.

On the other hand, the proliferation of television channels and news came at the same time as a decline in the audience for news programming. Cable and satellite penetration is nearly ubiquitous, and has increased even more because of the FCC-mandated switch to digital broadcasting in June 2009. Pair a steady loss of audience and advertising with an ever-expanding multi-channel broadcasting environment and the path leads to an increase in entertaining, inexpensive programming. It also yields more infotainment on TV news. An article in *Discourse & Society*, "The Infotainment Quotient in Routine Television News: A Director's Perspective," found that the framing of news stories became deliberately dramatic; and entertainment features often overshadowed the policy-relevant aspects of news. And a 1999 study by Jay Blumber and Dennis Kavanagh in *Political Communication* argues that a significant increase in competitive pressures, coupled with postmodern anti-elitist populism, transformed the way citizens received news and engaged with political issues:

> This is reflected not only in the explosion of subgenres designed as hybrids—breakfast shows, news magazines, talk shows, crime watches, tabloid television, and so forth—but also in the further mixing of information with drama, excitement, colour, and human interest in the topics, formats and styles.

Media critics, especially former journalists, say the 1990s marked a period of unprecedented decay in broadcast journalism. Historians David Marc and Robert Thompson suggest news stories "were little more than promotions for upcoming entertainment shows." And a 1997 study by the Project of Excellence in Journalism noted that, "there has been a shift toward lifestyle, celebrity, entertainment and celebrity crime/scandal in the news, and away from government and foreign affairs ... The greatest shift in emphasis of network news was a marked rise in the number of stories about scandals, up from one-half of 1 percent in 1977 to 15 percent in 1997."

Bill Kovach and Tom Rosenstiel also argue, in *Warp Speed: America in the Age of Mixed Media*, that profit-oriented journalism and the combination of infotainment and political spin had affected news agendas. They suggested four main reasons for this: (1) the 24/7 cycle with its appetite for live news; (2) the proliferation of news networks; (3) increasingly sophisticated methods of news management and the growing importance of "spin;" and (4) a ratings-driven news industry that promotes a "blockbuster mentality," privileging dramatic and entertainment reports over more staid forms of political news.

The evolution of infotainment has paralleled globalization of content and consolidation of ownership, especially since World War II. Critics say globalization has produced a cultural homogenization of media content. Global media culture is increasingly dominated by giant mega-corporations, which bring together TV, film, magazines, newspapers, books, information databases, computers, and other media, producing a "networked multimedia infotainment society." In the U.S., major news networks have acquired conglomerates whose primary interest is in the entertainment business—Viacom-Paramount owns CBS News; ABC News is part of the Disney Empire; GE owns NBC; CNN is a key component of AOL-Time Warner; and News Corporation owns Fox News, the *Wall Street Journal* and the *New York Post*. This shift in ownership is reflected in the type of stories—about celebrities from the world of entertainment—that often gets prominence on news. Stars of new Disney films appear on ABC News programs; Fox affiliates routinely feature *American Idol* "stories" in their local newscasts; and as mentioned before, the *Early Show* on CBS often devotes a portion of Friday's two-hour program to the latest *Survivor* episodes from the night before. By 2008, 10 mega-corporations controlled most of the production of information and entertainment throughout the globe, including the top 20 websites and important internet infrastructure. The result is less competition and diversity, and more corporate control of all media. And more infotainment.

Critics argue that the problem isn't (necessarily) ownership incursion into newsrooms. The problem is that infotainment finds its way into the news in much more subtle ways. Former broadcast journalist Bonnie Anderson skewers broadcast news for adding infotainment to add to the bottom line. Regardless of input from above, journalists increasingly fill their newscasts with salacious gossip and Hollywood promotions, not because the boss ordered them to but because celebrity sells. Noam Chomsky envisioned elements of power usurping media messages two decades ago with his critical treatise *Manufacturing Consent*, predicting that efforts at objectivity would leave journalists impotent against establishment messages. He was half right. Today's mainstream media has evolved from being a media watchdog against the powers that be to tail-wagging lapdog of entertainment self-promotion. In 2002, ABC tried to lure David Letterman to leave CBS for an earlier time slot—the 11:30 p.m. real estate occupied by ABC News *Nightline*. Letterman turned down the $31 million offer to avoid being "the guy who killed *Nightline*" with an entertainment program. But Ted Koppel had become a star in his own right over the show's two decades, earning $8 million that year. It becomes difficult to argue against the fusion of news and entertainment when CBS *Evening News* anchor Katie Couric commands a salary of $15 million a year.

Thussu argues that the global circulation of infotainment has undermined the public-service ethos of media, but at the same time a "global infotainment sphere is emerging as a potential site for competing versions of journalism, including an increasingly vocal and visible blogosphere."

MEDIA AND SOCIETY OF SPECTACLE

Classical Greece had its Olympics, its public rhetorical battles, and its violent wars. Ancient Rome had its orgies, its public offerings of bread and circuses, parades and monuments for triumphant Caesars and their armies. Machiavelli advised his modern prince about the usefulness of spectacle for government and social control. In *Bread and Circus: Theories of Social Decay*, Patrick Brantlinger found analogies between TV and Roman circuses:

> They both substitute immediate visual experience for anything deeper or less immediate; they both impinge from above or outside on mass audiences of non-participatory spectators; they both seem to substitute false experiences of community for something more general, and the sex and violence of commercial television appeals like the Roman games to sadomasochistic instincts.

The concept of the "society of spectacle" was first developed by French theorist Guy Debord and his colleagues in the Situationist International movement in the 1960s, and condensed in *La societe du spectacle*.

Spectacles become defining events of their era, and Kellner has developed an essential work interpreting and analyzing several of them from an American perspective. These megaspectacles not only include commodity spectacles such as McDonald's or Nike campaigns, but also such events as the 1991 Gulf War, the O.J. Simpson trials, the Clinton sex and impeachment scandals, the Princess Diana wedding, death and funeral, the U.S. presidential election in 2000, the 9/11 attacks, and the War on Terror that followed.

In a historic period defined by media spectacles and entertainment, cultural debates have been polarized: Is humanity becoming more stupid or has culture been democratized? Since the advent of mass media there has been a tension between "dumbing down" the public or raising them up, between informing and educating or entertaining the crowd, the will of the people or the good of the people, the dialectic between the market and the moral. Legendary media scholar Harold Lasswell argued, in 1947, that the role of the mass media was to survey the world, correlate it to one's self, and transmit that knowledge to succeeding generations. But sociologist Charles Wright added a vital new function in 1960—entertainment. In *Amusing Ourselves to Death: Public Discourse in the Age of Show Business*, Neil Postman formulated that public discourse in the United States was assuming the form of entertainment. He argued that the nature of TV militates against deeper knowledge and television's conversations promote "incoherence and triviality." "Television does not extend or amplify literate culture. It attacks it."

On Television and Journalism suggests that infotainment thrives on emotional appeal and irrational human impulses. At the same time, "TV news suits everybody because it confirms what they already know, and above all, leaves their mental structures intact." In *Citizens and Consumers*, Garcia Canclini wrote, "Argumentative and critical forms of participation cede their place to the pleasure taken in electronic media spectacles where narration or the simple accumulation of anecdotes prevails over reasoned solutions to problems."

Daya Thussu argues that there is a pressing need to go beyond the debate about "dumbing down." For Thussu,:

> Infotainment entails much more than dumbing down: it works as a powerful discourse of diversion, in both senses, taking the attention away from, and displacing from the airwaves, such grim realities of neo-liberal imperialism as witnessed in the US invasion and occupation of Iraq, the intellectual and cultural subjugation by the tyranny of technology; of free market capitalism and globalization of a profligate and unsustainable consumerist lifestyle.

On the other hand, supporters of popular communication paradigms have tended to valorize the rise of infotainment suggesting that it expands and democratizes the public sphere. As evidenced by the penny press, historians have argued that sex, scandal, disaster, and celebrity have been intrinsic to modern journalism since the beginning, and discourses on "dumbing down" and "tabloidization" just represent elitist views of news. Others have also criticized this idealized view of "high modern journalism" and highlight the idea that making political communication appealing could generate more interest in civic affairs, contributing to a more democratic and inclusive media. Enter *The Daily Show* and *Saturday Night Live*. This new model of hybrid news and entertainment is frowned upon by traditional journalists—but they may be missing the point. Young adults are much more likely to watch news satire than news. If the humor is funnier to the informed viewer, perhaps the viewer will be compelled to become more informed. Given the diversity of "channels" available to today's content producers and consumers, there is room for hard news, soft news and fake news.

CRITICAL INFOTAINMENT

Boundaries between news and entertainment, and between public affairs and pop culture have become difficult to discern. It seems true that quality journalism, especially in broadcasting, is scarce and infotainment is a mainstay of contemporary media. While it can promote relativism and stupidity, it can also promote critical, progressive, and even subversive causes in society.

As Chapter 2 details, audiences for news fell considerably in the past few decades, and the sharpest decline came among young people. A 2004 Pew Research Center study found that 34 percent of young people (ages 18-29) are turning to another form of news—late night television and comedy shows. During the 2008 election, it was 60 percent—and nearly half of all adults cited news satire as a source for campaign information.

Comedy Central's *The Daily Show* has been called "young America's news source" and its host, Jon Stewart, "the most trusted name in fake news." It has become a media phenomenon in the United States, and an essential force in American political communication. The half-hour show offers a satiric interpretation of politics and current events in which Stewart mocks both those who make and report the news. It features a cast of "correspondents" and includes interviews with celebrities, politicians or media people. Its hybrid blend of comedy, news, and political conversation has proven to be a success in terms of audiences and influence. For Geoffrey Baym in the *Daily Show: Discursive Integration and the Reinvention of Political Journalism*, the use of parody unmasks the artifice in much contemporary news practices, while the interview segment endorses and enacts a deliberative model of democracy based on civility of exchange, complexity of argument and the goal of mutual understanding—along with copious laughs. In a time when most media have turned to shallow infotainment to try to bolster ratings, *The Daily Show* offers instead a version of news that entertains.

The Daily Show attracts many young people with its initial discourse of entertainment. A number of scholars have found that while young people do want to be entertained, they also want to be informed. In *The News about Comedy*, Lauren Feldman notes that the show's use of irony and satire does more than inject emotion and subjectivity into the news; it implies a shared understanding between communicator and receiver. In this sense, the show might encourage young viewers to tune into traditional forms of news, or to seek more information online, so that they have the context necessary to appreciate the program's humor. In fact, the 2004 National Annenberg Election Survey found that young people who watch *The Daily Show* are also more knowledgeable about politics than non-viewers.

For Baym, comedy also provides the method to engage in serious political criticism. The label of "fake news" frees the show to say what traditional journalism cannot. "Never claiming to be news, it can hardly be charged with being illegitimate journalism, either by the political structure it interrogates or the news media it threatens." Lauren Feldman thinks satire doesn't so much challenge the legitimacy of serious news as it challenges the news media to think more responsibly about what journalism should look like today. Feldman observes that some have begun to re-evaluate notions of professional practice like objectivity, so that comedy and entertainment might not be incompatible with substantive journalism. The pitfall is whether journalistic responsibility can be successfully negotiated in a media world where comedians—who resist any claim to accountability—are reporting the news.

Baym thinks *The Daily Show* can be better understood not as "fake news" but as an experiment in journalism, an alternative journalism that uses satire to interrogate power, parody to critique contemporary news, and funny dialogue as a model of deliberative democracy. Discourses of news, politics, entertainment and marketing have grown deeply inseparable with each making inroads into the realm of the other.

While *The Daily Show* presents an entertaining alternative to mainstream media it is, still, part of a media conglomeration—Canada's CTV Globe. *The Daily* Show is also, clearly, not the first attempt at news satire. The satirical magazine *The Onion* has been around since 1988, providing daily skewers of mainstream news and newsmakers. In the last decade, alternative publications in Latin America have also used these resources to develop social, political, and cultural criticism and exorcize collective traumas. *The Clinic* offered non-mainstream points of view about society after the Pinochet dictatorship in Chile and *Barcelona* tackled the 2001 economic crisis is Argentina.

So "critical infotainment" is not new. Satire, parody, acid humor, and other subversive forms have a long, ancient tradition in human communication, and diverse references according to the local contexts and historic periods in which they are developed. Nevertheless, as a Peruvian poet once wrote: "Everything has already been said. But as nobody listens, we'll have to say it again."

"Critical infotainment" may have no more lively a home than in today's digital media environment, which promises the skewering of news from organizations like Comedy Central down to individual bloggers. The multimedia landscape laid bare by digital technology promises to generate a wealth of alternative media projects, blending genres—journalism, entertainment, satire, and popular culture—and narratives—text, video, audio, and photos. The future of news may be unrecognizable to the occupants of the legacy media's Ivory towers, but it will probably make you laugh.

THE ALTERNATIVE PRESS

"Alternative media is almost oxymoronic. Everything is, at some point, alternative to something else."

—John Downing

Media spectacle, ownership conglomeration, abdication to public relations, allegations of bias—no wonder the mainstream news media are losing the trust of today's audiences. It seems that the fate of journalism has fallen into the hands of the highest bidder. Claiming to be the antithesis of the mainstream news media, alternative news steps onto the scene, claiming to provide a breath of fresh air—greater diversity in news coverage and a renewed focus on the issues that really matter to audiences. In January 1998, Matt Drudge, then a no-name employee at the CBS studios gift shop in Hollywood, broke the story of the decade when he revealed the Monica Lewinsky scandal on his website. A story that led to the impeachment trial of President Clinton did not originate behind flashy anchor desks or major news networks websites but from a guy with a computer his father had bought for him. A few months later, Drudge spoke at the National Press Club and asked all the professional reporters listening, "How did a story like Monica Lewinsky break out of a Hollywood apartment? What does that say about the Washington press corps? It just baffles me. I haven't come up with answers on that." And the crowd applauded—the same crowd of journalists who were aware of the story but ignored it until they were forced into a corner to report it.

These kinds of events are part of the driving force behind alternative media's popularity. No gatekeepers, no layers of editors, and no filters on information. This empowers the individual by allowing a free flow of information. Thus, it's with some irony that we watch the beleaguered state of mainstream media in the digital age: Even as technology becomes more advanced, the few mass media companies that control most print, broadcast and online news media have come to appear more backward than ever in their governing structure and bureaucratic operations. Mitzi Waltz has noted that the level of monopoly on content and access mirrors backward to governments from centuries ago and could be attributed to the driving force behind the growth of alternative media. These media giants armed with supreme financial power are able to amass vast political power so that laws are amended to work in their favor. In one recent example, the Federal Communications Commission in 2003 voted to allow media conglomerates to purchase more television stations, newspapers and other broadcast outlets in the same city.

Lowry Mays, the founder of Clear Channel, summed it up best about the media conglomerates when he said, "We're not in the business of providing news and information. We're not in the business of providing well-researched music. We're simply in the business of selling our customers products." Clear Channel has also been accused of firing anyone with political opinions that differ from their own. For example, when the United States was on the verge of invading Afghanistan after the Sept. 11 attacks in 2001, Davey D, the host of a popular talk radio show, aired an interview with Barbara Lee, the only member of the U.S. Congress to vote against the invasion. Davey D's radio station, KMEL in San Francisco, had been recently purchased by Clear Channel. He was fired, and company executives sent a memo to all of Clear

Channel's stations warning them not to play any songs that would contradict support for the U.S.-led invasion, such as John Lennon's "Imagine."

WHAT EXACTLY IS THE ALTERNATIVE PRESS?

One woman's alternative is another's mainstream, hence the difficulty in pinning down a precise representation of "alternative press." A basic definition would simply be media that are in *opposition* to mainstream news media. But, according to Mitzi Waltz, author of *Alternative and Activist Media*, what is mainstream to one society is considered alternative to another. She gives the example of CNN in North Korea, a country where all outside media is banned. CNN, a major mainstream news media in the U.S. and several other parts of the world, is instead considered an alternative news media in North Korea because of its opposition to state propaganda. The wider debate on what constitutes alternative media continues to include blogs, forums on personal websites, news that target only a select group in the community (gays and lesbians, golfers, musicians, etc.), and many other news outlets that can be considered alternative news as well. There are even a number of high-profile blogs that cover journalism, including a mix of new media upstarts (MediaMemo, Gawker, Media Bistro) and old media migrating online (Nieman Journalism Lab, Poynter Institute, *Columbia Journalism Review, Editor & Publisher*).

It is important to distinguish between early and current definitions of alternative media in a now-mature online age. A decade ago, an online news presence *was* alternative. Today, scholars and journalists alike comfortably define mainstream media, online or off (in print or on TV), together—as they should. The citizen journalist, audience member responding to a report, or a woman challenging bank fees by posting her protest on YouTube all are alternatives by traditional definitions. But that doesn't mean they aren't journalists.

Media theorists have long battled for a suitable definition of alternative media. Richard Abel, a law professor at UCLA, has claimed that it is impossible to define alternative media. Michael Albert, one of the founders of radical left media group Z Communications, has argued that alternative media cannot simply be a product that differs from the mainstream in content but must also be different in how it functions and organizes as an institution. Chris Atton, a leading international scholar on alternative media, has several different sets of criteria to gauge whether the content is alternative or not. In the end, no consensus has been reached.

Contrary to popular beliefs, it is not accurate to claim that alternative news media are completely in opposition to mainstream news media, although several alternative news sources claim to be. Raymond Williams, a Welsh academic whose work in cultural studies became the foundations in the field, makes a vital distinction between *alternative* and *oppositional* viewpoints. An alternative viewpoint is one that seeks to coexist within the existing hegemony, but an oppositional viewpoint aims to replace it. It is hard to decipher whether most alternative news' main goal is to replace the hegemonic news industry or to play more of a watchdog role. Many alternative news websites condemn the work of mainstream news media, but they rely on the mainstream's content as fodder for their critiques.

Since there is no one tidy definition, for the purposes of this chapter alternative media are defined by their approach to news. That is, they may cover the same topics as the mainstream media, but they do so with different priorities, perspectives and/or reactionary analyses.

SAVED BY THE WEB

We tend to think of the alternative press as a recent development, perhaps in large part because it has garnered greater attention and readers online. However, alternative media have long been in existence: Indeed, as long as there has been a "mainstream" press, there have been media in opposition to them. Around the beginning of the 20th century, the hunger for alternative information led to muckraking exposés of the U.S. meat packing industry, Rockefeller's monopolization of the oil industry, and of the shame of lynching and poverty. In the 1960s and early 70s, the third wave of feminists decided that if they were going to be heard, it was not going to be through the mainstream press—they would have to publish their own papers. And for well more than a century, the alternative press has disseminated the voice of anti-war activists.

But, through it all, alternative media were called the "underground press" for a reason—their influence was often obscured in public discourse. There was still the cost of economy of scale. After all, as much as 80 percent of newspaper costs stem from production and distribution. And for the truly nefarious, a single printing press is easy to stop. Enter the internet, which may well be the saving grace for the alternative movement and its media. Thanks to this far-reaching, low-cost medium, alternative media not only have shed their pariah status, but they have become hip and ever more effective in disseminating their message. Instead of trying to compete with corporations' slick marketing, alternative media have bypassed traditional channels to set up inexpensive websites that are nevertheless effective in reaching a distributed base of activists, and in attracting a wider audience through search engines and outreach online.

Thus, unlike mainstream news media's declining fortunes and dwindling audiences, alternative news media are thriving online. A recent Project for Excellence in Journalism's State of the News Media report found that one of the most promising areas for audience growth was alternative weekly newspaper websites and the online audience numbers continued to grow across media outlets. The website network Village Voice Media, which also owns *Village Voice* in New York and 15 other alternative weeklies in major cities across the country, had the 10th-most visited newspaper site in November 2007, according to *Editor and Publisher*. The company's online audience increased 127 percent in one year and the total time spent on its sites increased 89 percent. Pew also found that more than one in three Americans visits blogs; one in ten posts. One in twelve engage in social networking with a mobile device, like a wireless phone. And all of them read, follow and post without having to pass through an editor.

Gone are the days of god-like journalism—when whatever was printed in the newspaper or reported on the television news was gospel to its readers. Now audiences demand more viewpoints, and alternative press is no longer the castaway cousin of the mainstream media. It is now trendy and hip to be able to log on to the internet and be served with an array of opinions and perspectives. Once considered the domain of society's oddballs, alternative media have gained the respect of many. Whereas the dissemination of alternative news and information used to be difficult because the audience was so diffuse, now the internet has made such information easily and globally accessible. Unlike mainstream media where the reports are only from a select few, the internet allows virtually unlimited space for alternative viewpoints.

JOURNALISM'S WATCHDOG

The alternative media have enjoyed this renaissance in part because of their adversarial role as a watchdog for journalism—a check against the mainstream press. The alternative press can claim the moral high ground in large because of their independence from corporate management and from advertisers who might silence unwanted news. Indeed, one of the alternative media's most popular appeals is that it does not have to answer to a "higher power"—including the professional journalistic pretense of objectivity. Alternative media are anything but neutral, on purpose.

Neutrality in mainstream news now is perceived as boring at the least, unappreciated at the most. Mainstream news now often serve as the preface to alternative news content. Audiences obtain the mainstream news to get the gist of things but proceed to alternative news media to obtain more in-depth analysis, opinions or perspectives that the mainstream news does not offer. Bloggers were vibrantly active in the 2008 presidential election and, in fact, the White House blog was updated to read "Change has come to America" at the instant Barack Obama was sworn in. Facebook was alive with updated posts at the historic moment, supporting and decrying the president. And CNN then covered the bloggers, on the air and online.

According to Nigel Parry, "alternative" or "supplementary" news are gaining popularity especially because of the current global political tensions. Just 9 percent of news consumers got political information online in 2000. By 2008 it was 28 percent. AlterNet.org, the most popular alternative news website according to Alexa (a web information company that tracks traffic on several websites) has seen a gradual increase in audience reception over the past three years.

Media consumers today are savvier than ever. From cell phones to gaming consoles, one is able to get the news almost anywhere today. With this bombardment of technology delivering news into so many different mediums, audiences cannot help but be trained to the fact that there is more than one side to each news report. In the wake of the 9/11 tragedy, *The Guardian* newspaper reported that traffic from the U.K. to Middle Eastern news websites surged as media users sought out alternative news sources to supplement their local news reports.

In this world where everything is fast becoming personalized, audiences want their news to be personalized as well. There are audiences who want to read different perspectives not available in the mainstream press and there are audiences who want to read from others who share their same opinions. Either way the alternative press offers them both options. Readers seem to enjoy the passion that is inherent in alternative news. They enjoy uncovering reports not found in the mainstream, and like digging deeper into those issues shallowly reported. Perhaps alternative news can be more aggressive and freewheeling because of its very nature: By being alternative, such media have an almost invisible safety net. If the alternative news media's assumptions prove to be accurate, kudos to them—if they happen to be inaccurate, they are not held to the same standards or expectations of the mainstream news media.

CHALLENGES FOR THE ALTERNATIVE PRESS

But, going forward, can the alternative press of the future retain its alternative spirit? Consider the *Village Voice*, which began heavy on political content but now features mostly happenings in New York City, laden with fashion, gossip and restaurant reviews—and the occasional news piece thrown in there. The *Village Voice* was bought by Rupert Murdoch in 1977 and has since gone through a slew of corporate owners. The *San Francisco Bay Guardian*, one of the pioneers in local alternative journalism, has now taken on a similar route, its content primarily focused on soft news and reviews of restaurants, movies and music. These alternative weeklies have perhaps been victims of their own success, shifting to delivering an elusive and highly attractive audience to advertisers. As Sean Elder wrote in Salon.com, "It's a demographic of college-educated people in their early 30s making $40K and up … . Media money men see the weekly giveaway paper as a reader-magnet, stuffed with classifieds, personals and ads for 'massage' providers."

According to Comedia, adopting a capitalist model is essential for media hoping to break out of the "alternative ghetto" of obscurity—"an existence so marginal as to be irrelevant." But is it too idealistic to believe that alternative media cannot function and grow without corporate-style structure and organization? It is no easy feat trying to mirror the mainstream press (in managerial practice) and yet criticize their content at the same time. Perhaps a better way for alternative journalists to grow and flourish is to reposition themselves as supplementing the mainstream news—reporting where the mainstream media has left off—rather than trying to supplant them. There is tremendous potential influence in this infinite independence. Think of Medusa—a multi-headed being that answers to no one. New York University professor Clay Shirky embraces the shifting sands of crowd sourcing, crowd reporting, and crowd funding in his aptly named book, *Here Comes Everybody: The Power of Organizing Without Organizations*. Iranian citizens mobilized online after the 2009 elections heavily favored incumbent Mahmoud Ahmadinejad despite polls hinting he would lose. The pen may be mightier than the sword—but cell phone video trumped them both, flooding YouTube with damning video of crushing government responses to protests. Again, CNN embraced and ran the video on the air, another case of the mainstream following the alternative.

Meanwhile, one of the greatest traits of alternative news media is also one of its greatest challenges—diversity. No two alternative news websites are as similar as most of the mainstream news websites. This can be useful in providing an array of voices, but also difficult in offering a coherent message or call for social action. It also brings a measure of capitalism into a realm that was traditionally loath to embrace it. Those sites that best serve their audience—even an alternative audience—find themselves at the center of a network of ideas.

Likewise, the term "alternative" itself is so elastic that it can be devoid of any real meaning, as Richard Abel has observed. Alternative media cannot be everything that the local news is not. At present, alternative media are virtually structure-less. There are no guidelines, no guild, and the only fraternity that is closest to an "alternative" association is the Association of Alternative Newsweeklies (AAN). With no cohesion among the people who are associated with alternative press, it is difficult to have common goals and track progress. *Alternatives in Print* (the current major bibliographical reference work in this field) presents three simple criteria against which to test the publishers that appear in their pages. They deem a publisher as an alternative one if it meets at least one of these criteria:

1. The publisher has to be non-commercial, demonstrating that "a basic concern for ideas, not the concern for profit, is the motivation for publication."
2. The subject matter of their publications should focus on "social responsibility or creative expression, or usually a combination of both."
3. Finally, it is enough for publishers to define themselves as alternative publishers.

Ironically, these criteria apply nicely to a "new mainstream" media taking shape in the ether of the new media environment. *Nieman Reports* dedicated an entire 2009 issue to the amorphous media, showcasing a half-dozen new nonprofit models that embrace crowdfunding or live on philanthropy. Each of them, from the St. Louis Beacon to the Voice of San Diego to Spot.us, is non-commercial, dedicated to socially responsible coverage, and might be defined as alternative—but alternative to what, exactly?

The lack of cohesion in all phases of the alternative press—from organizational fuzziness to diffuse messages to unclear linkages among alternative media—call for action to prevent the movement from flaming out so soon after it has flourished in the digital era. Indeed, the history of the alternative press has been one of boom and bust, birth, death and rebirth. The unique technological and cultural setting of the internet, however, offers hope for a robust and sustained period of alternative media.

FUTURE OF ALTERNATIVE NEWS

Looking ahead, we can imagine alternative news growing because the internet has paved the way for its growth. Though not a foolproof journey, the web has cleared many hurdles impossible to overcome without the internet. Financial deterrents are not so much a concern now and the convenience of the internet is unsurpassable. The alternative press will take on more responsibilities as the mainstream media's watchdog. They will report on what the mainstream news media failed to include and offer deeper and different analysis.

Mainstream news media will be left with no choice but to pay more attention to the perspectives and stories that the alternative press covers. Mainstream news media will have to come up with better explanations when questioned why certain stories or perspectives did not make their news. The quest to discredit alternative news will be intensified, although the mainstream news will not have to explain opinions from the alternative side as they are merely that—opinions and not facts. Mainstream news will be unable to have the freedom that alternative news enjoy as they are owned by big media conglomerates and must answer to the upper management. For example, if Disney were to be caught in a monumental scandal, it would be difficult, if not impossible, for the ABC news channels to report it fairly without fear of repercussions. Then again, in the months after the September 11 terrorist attacks, one-third of Americans believed the Bush Administration played some role in the attacks—a belief roundly reported on websites from Prison Planet to YouTube.

Mainstream news may never have the same kind of appeal as alternative news because it is a profit-driven institution that will always try to cater to the masses. Alternative news, on the other hand, will cater to many different niche audiences, and are often nonprofits. The alternative press' identity would already be revealed to its audience beforehand. Its political leanings and fundamental ideas would have been publicized. The mainstream news, meanwhile, should not possess any sort of biased identity other than a completely neutral one lest they jeopardize their quest for bias-free reporting.

A STRONGER FUTURE

Going forward, alternative media are poised to become a more prominent and important watchdog for journalism, assuming they can overcome a few key obstacles. First, a solid definition needs to be in place to determine what exactly encompasses alternative news media. Although there will never be a definition that will be satisfactory to everyone, there must at least be a wide general consensus as to the definition of alternative news media. With a widely accepted definition, goals and associations may be established to form cohesion among those in the alternative media to strengthen its role in the media world.

Second, after a consensus is reached for the definition of alternative news media, research must be conducted to understand whom these audiences of alternative news are. There are sundry articles dedicated to mainstream news media's audience but hardly any to understand the alternative media's consumers. It is more than likely that alternative news audiences are also mainstream news audiences, so it would also be crucial to determine how much of each genre they consume, the reasons for seeking out an alternative news source (or the reasons for *avoiding* seeking alternative news sources) and the differences that are distinct to each group.

Unlike mainstream media's agenda, which has been researched repeatedly, the alternative media's agenda has yet to be fully explored. One of the problems is the complicated definition of what encompasses alternative media and the different agendas each alternative media outlet possesses. Although each mainstream news media may differ slightly in what it believes to be the most important news (depending on medium and locale), there is a general consensus that certain topics will trump other stories each time. However, with alternative news media there is no such consensus because each outlet is championing its own agenda or theme.

It is easier to conduct research—but not necessarily in the best interest of media consumers—when mainstream news media report relatively the same news with the same angle. One of the crucial points for furthering the understanding of alternative news media is to find out who are its audiences and what do they read and why. Chris Atton, the alternative media guru, conducted a small-scale survey of about 50 self-selected respondents who read alternative news and the results suggested that people seek out alternative media because they want mobilizing information and want to be informed of news that are ignored or marginalized by the mainstream media. However, this survey was conducted in 1999. The climate of news information has been rapidly evolving and a newer, more representative survey is due.

More detailed analyses must be conducted in the near future with the most popular alternative news sources to investigate the agendas they are setting and the audiences they attract. Although assumptions are that alternative news media still cannot completely replace mainstream news media, there is no denying that the growth of alternative news will continue to rise as the internet continues to provide one of the most inexpensive and most efficient ways in distributing to a large, international audience. Perhaps most importantly, the voice of those watching the watchdogs—the mainstream media—has never been more robust. "I'm a fake journalist, and I'm embarrassed these guys scooped me," said the *Daily Show's* Stewart. "Let's get to work people."

SUGGESTED READING

Atton, Chris. (2002). *Alternative Media*. Great Britain: Athenaeum Press.

Couldry, Nick & Curran, James (2003). *Contesting Media Power: Alternative media in a networked world*. Maryland: Rowman & Littlefield Publishers.

Debord, Guy (1977). *The Society of Spectacle*. Detroit: Red and Black. First published in 1967 as *La societe du spetacle* by Buchet-Chastel, Paris.

Kellner, Douglas (2003). *Media Culture and the Triumph of The Spectacle*. New York: Routledge.

Thussu, Daya (2007) *News as Entertainment: The Rise of Global Infotainment*. New York: Sage Publications.

Waltz, Mitzi (2006). *Alternative and Activist Media*. New York: Columbia University Press

Chapter 8

Social Media and News as User Experience

Cindy Royal

THE RISE OF online social networking has had a dramatic effect on interpersonal communication patterns, so it is no surprise that it is also affecting news dissemination and the processes of media organizations. Most people who use social networking sites have little insight into the professional uses and profound changes that these spaces are making in the world of media. Quite often, they are viewed as time-wasting and frivolous, but their value to journalism and democracy is slowly being recognized.

Social networking, as defined by researchers danah boyd and Nicole Ellison, is "web-based services that allow individuals to (1) construct a public or semi-public profile within a bounded system, (2) articulate a list of other users with whom they share a connection, and (3) view and traverse their list of connections and those made by others within the system." Social networking possesses characteristics that have been available since the early internet. Message boards, discussion groups, email, chat, recommendations and user comments have long been a regular part of internet culture. Social networks are simply more elaborate ways to help people make connections and perform these activities using technologies known commonly as Web 2.0. Popular sites like MySpace and Facebook provide a platform for millions of users to interact with friends, share links and upload photos and videos. Micro-blogging sites like Twitter let users broadcast their day-to-day activities, along with links to articles they are reading and photos, to those that follow them. And news aggregator Digg has revolutionized the way in which information comes to the fore, by a popular vote of online users, rather than by being selected by a handful of powerful editors and mainstream media outlets. This chapter will further define the social networking space and its relevance to communication theory and the journalism profession and then will provide examples of how news organizations are engaging users and building community. Finally, suggestions for how social media environments may be developed, measured and valued will be offered.

UNDERSTANDING THE SOCIAL NETWORKING SPACE

Many social networking sites have quickly become part of the fabric of internet culture and daily life, receiving millions of visitors per month. They are all phenomena of the new millennium, started mostly by young tech entrepreneurs. Facebook, started in 2004, initially invited users associated with a university community (its founder Mark Zuckerberg launched the site when he was a Harvard undergraduate) to interact with friends and engage in relationships. It is now open to all users. MySpace, started in 2003, whose early inhabitants were bands and musical groups seeking ways to share music and announce engagements, has grown to one of the most popular spaces on the web. It allows users to set up a web presence and to communicate with those in their network of friends. Purchased by News Corporation, the owners of Fox Broadcasting, MySpace has slowed in growth in recent years. YouTube, started in 2005, is a space for uploading videos and for user discussion of multimedia content. And Twitter, which began in 2006, has quickly brought the microblogging platform to the forefront of social media discussions. Of the 1.1 billion people age 15 and older worldwide who accessed the internet from a home or work location in May 2009, 734 million visited at least one social networking site during the month—65% of the worldwide internet audience. The worldwide audience for social networking sites has been growing 25% per year since 2007. Although rankings may change within the social networking space, there is no question that the popularity of these sites in general has reached a critical mass and continues to grow.

While each of these sites has a unique business model and demographics, the characteristic of user-generated content is common across all social networking spaces and is critical to their popularity and success. Sometimes that content is in the form of personal blog posts or status messages. But increasingly users on social networking sites are sharing photos, uploading videos and commenting on and posted items from other media. The conversations are broad, far-reaching and individualized. And they are slowly influencing the ways that traditional media distribute and report news.

Understanding the ways that users are contributing content on social networks holds particular importance to the world of journalism. The concept of citizen journalism is a likely area for these concepts to be explored, but with major news sites, including *USA Today* implementing social networking characteristics, such as rating stories and creating discussion groups around coverage, the ideas around social networking become more relevant in regard to regular engagement with news media. No longer simply a passing trend for young internet users, social networking has grown to mainstream usage and acceptance. But, until recently, most newspapers had done little in terms of using these features to more formally engage readers. Providing tools for social networking is one thing. The biggest challenge comes in encouraging reader participation and driving the contributions of those readers to your site. News consumers receive news from a plethora of online sources, including aggregators like Yahoo, Google and Digg, and a host of blogs. Craigslist is a social network supplanting classified ads that used to be the sole domain of the newspaper business. Social networking provides many opportunities, and shows no signs of disappearing or being relegated to a fad.

Newspapers have been considering the social aspects of news for several years. In a *Wired* article, Ralph Terkowitz, vice president of technology at the *Washington Post*, said the paper is interested in exploring new ways of "helping readers to communicate with the paper and each other." Terkowitz mentioned possible features including discussion groups devoted to world politics virtual book clubs. He also mentioned user-generated classified ads. "There are a number of ways it could be used to reach under-served segments of the newspaper marketplace," he said. "We are very excited about the service and what it could do."

According to a Pew Center study, young people who are savvy with technology, known as "digital natives," are frequently creating and contributing online content. The study reported that "more than half of American teenagers have created a blog, posted an artistic or written creation online, helped build a website, created an online profile, or uploaded photos and videos to a website." This trend reflects not only an opportunity, but an expectation on the part of young people to participate in content creation, not to simply consume it. As young people are turning away from reading traditional newspapers, this presents a means by which young audiences can have their interest in news and information reinvigorated.

The relevance to communication theory comes in its engagement with traditional theories, made current with new media technologies. The uses and gratifications line of theory has long differentiated between what media did to people and what people do with media. Studies in this area seek to understand why people use media, and why they make certain choices about media in their lives. The process is considered active. In 1972 McQuail et al. wrote "media use is most suitably characterized as an interactive process, relating media content, individual needs, perceptions, roles and values and the social context in which a person is situated." But, the meaning of the term "interactive" has changed significantly since this time, when media choice was approached as a process that was actively influenced by a variety of factors. Now, when we speak of using media interactively, we are discussing the two-way communication features of social media and the concept of user-generated content.

The emergence of computer-mediated communication has re-energized the application of uses and gratifications theories in studying media. According to Thomas Ruggiero, "Uses and gratifications has always provided a cutting-edge theoretical approach in the initial stages of each new mass communications medium: newspapers, radio and television, and now the internet. Although scientists are likely to continue using traditional tools and typologies to answer questions about media use, we must also be prepared to expand our current theoretical models of uses and gratifications."

The internet, now driven by Web 2.0 technologies that enable collaboration and sharing, has fostered a new age of participation. In *Convergence Culture: Where Old and New Media Collide,* Henry Jenkins studied the themes of media convergence, participatory culture, and collective intelligence. Driven by digital technologies, Jenkins described a world that is bound not by a particular medium or industry, but one in which consumer and producer are merged, and culture is created by means of sharing and participation. With the internet as the primary driver, consumers of culture are able to participate in ways that are both sanctioned and non-sanctioned by powerful media industries.

These online tools, in most cases originated to facilitate interpersonal communication, are increasingly being co-opted by news organizations. The concept of news itself is being redefined as "hyperlocal" when news is as much about what your friends are doing right now as it is about the latest national and international coverage. And increasingly, breaking news is more quickly disseminated on these online platforms than in their traditional media counterparts. With the increasing usage and reliance on mobile platforms, such as the iPhone, users expect their news to be delivered anywhere, on demand, and with special applications (iPhone apps) and increasingly expect to be involved in the process via contribution and engagement. News outlets are competing for the attention of consumers with a broad range of professional and amateur communicators, and some are trying innovative ways to engage the modern news consumer.

ENGAGING USERS

We are only at the beginning of understanding ways in which news organizations can use social media tools to engage their audiences. Many news sites allow for comments on news stories, offer blogs that allow for user contributions across a wide range of categories including sports, pets and entertainment, and provide users the opportunity to share personal photos and videos. Some are experimenting with Digg-type rating systems that measure the popularity of stories or provide tools that allow users to easily share articles. And, some organizations are using the micro-blogging platform Twitter to drive traffic to their stories, engage the public as sources, and to present a more personal side of their staff.

Due to the increased expectation of participation on the part of the user, news organizations are beginning to understand their role beyond that of content provider to that of architect of user experience (UX). The concept of UX was an emerging issue at the annual South by Southwest Interactive Conference in 2009. Where "content is king" was once the mantra of online publishing platforms, it now seems to have been replaced by "UX is king." But, what exactly is meant by "user experience"? Like the terms "convergence" and "new media," its definition varies in context. It's a tough concept for people to grasp, particularly journalists, who traditionally have had control over almost every aspect of newspaper consumption, other than actually turning pages for readers. Designers have a general understanding of user experience in regard to usability and accessibility standards in terms of making a website that has proper functionality, design and navigation that can be accessed by a wide range of users, including those with disabilities. But increasingly, when UX is discussed, it is about what users can do online, encompassing design, content and functionality.

The social networking sites, like Facebook, MySpace, LinkedIn, Twitter and YouTube, have been very influential in this regard. Through these interactions, users are gaining an expectation of participation, regardless of their location or platform of access. And, while users don't necessarily seek monetary compensation for their participation (they seem to derive other forms of social capital from the experience), it is unlikely that they will be willing to pay for content that they are helping to create and publish. Combine this with consumers being accustomed to getting news for free and for having many free alternatives to traditional media content, and the chances of ever being able to charge for the majority of online content (either through subscriptions or micro-payments) become close to nil.

First, it may be helpful to understand what the user experience might look like for a news site. One of the best examples to date is the way in which the *New York Times* is engaging audiences with its data-driven interactives and WordTrain phrase presentations, delivering news as a two-way experience. For example, the *Times*' "Is It Better to Buy or Rent?" interactive graphic offers the user a completely customizable experience in understanding the factors involved in the decision to rent or buy a home. One could envision how a traditional story about renting versus buying would be written: interview a few people about their decision process, get some anecdotes, talk to a few experts. But, the individual reader would be left to factor their own variables and make a decision. The *New York Times* interactive provides a tool that helps the user customize their own version of the story, modifying variables and making assumptions relevant to their personal situation.

A more recent interactive plots New York City homicides on a map, providing information about the date, time of day, victim, perpetrator and weapon used. The map can be filtered on numerous variables, allowing the user to customize the story for their own neighborhood or workplace and to understand some of the elements that influence the propagation of crime. Often, the interactives are accompanied by full stories, as in the case of the homicide map, with an article about crime rising during summer months. But the story takes on new dimensions when users are allowed to work with the data and engage it on their own terms.

The *New York Times* is also an innovator in a form of crowdsourcing a story via its WordTrain feature. On election night, users were asked to submit one word that described how they felt. The only other piece of data that was collected was their party affiliation. Then the story of the night unfolded as users were able to watch the most prominent terms march across the screen in a visualization. Another popular WordTrain asked users about their feelings regarding the economy and their employment status. The data requirement, and thus the users' participation, is minimal, much like the parsimony of Twitter's 140-character limit. But the result is an astounding look at the pulse of an audience's sentiment.

The *New York Times* recently unveiled *Times* Wire, a Twitter-like feed that pushes short summaries and links to articles based on user preferences, and *Times* Reader 2.0, a desktop application that downloads stories and presents them in columnar format. The *Times* is also experimenting with different mobile formats including iPhone applications and is one of three newspapers that are in partnership with Amazon to subsidize the price of the Kindle e-book reader.

The term "hyperlocal" also relates to the user experience as news becomes redefined as anything that is of local interest. Our idea of news now includes what our family and friends are doing, along with interesting links, as well as local, national and international stories. Everyblock.com is a project created by former *Washington Post* journalist/developer Adrian Holovaty and funded by the Knight News Challenge that allows users to engage with and contribute to hyperlocal information based on their exact location. News becomes items like restaurant reviews and sanitation ratings, neighborhood events, local crime statistics and blog commentary. And, Everyblock.com has recently announced an iPhone app that makes the hyperlocal experience position-specific, engaging GPS to make the information relative to the user's exact location.

BUILDING COMMUNITY

Other features that are influencing news engagement are Digg-type popularity ratings, social media services that facilitate link sharing, and blog comments. And, many news organizations are going off their platform and engaging tools like Twitter to present news and information in a way that is personal and timely. The *Austin American-Statesman*'s Twitter account (@statesman) is much more than a simple RSS feed of stories. The main proprietor of the account uses it to promote stories, break news, get feedback and reply to users, often in a way that promotes a personal side to the publication. This activity takes place outside of the newspapers' main online presence. Some organizations have created Twitter accounts that utilize a mascot character to communicate with their audience, like the Chicago Tribune's Colonel Tribune (@ColonelTribune) and the Wilmington Star-News' Captain Star News (@CaptainStarNews). Twitter offers a variety of ways to repurpose its platform, by embedding RSS feeds or widgets of streams or by using its real-time search capabilities to search tweets (what Twitter uses have come to call their posts on the service) for trending topics and up-to-the-minute sentiment.

Twitter, often derided as a time waster and home to frivolous drivel of the masses, has demonstrated notable ways in which it has proven its value as an important information-dissemination device. On Jan. 15, 2009, a U.S. Airways plane made an emergency landing on the Hudson River after a dual engine failure caused by a bird strike. The pilot Capt. Chesley "Sully" Sullenberger was lauded as a hero after he safely landed the aircraft and all passengers were rescued by boats and ferries in the vicinity. The first photo at the scene and then disseminated quickly around the world was one taken on an iPhone by ferry passenger Janis Krums (@jkrums) [see http://twitpic.com/135xa]. He twittered this line along with the photo, "There's a plane in the Hudson. I'm on the ferry going to pick up the people. Crazy." He had only Twittered minutes before about wanting to get out of the city early that day to beat traffic. This photo, while not of professional quality, was the first image that most people saw of the aircraft and provided a personal perspective as the story unfolded on both legacy and social media platforms.

Probably the most effective and groundbreaking use of Twitter has been in the way it allowed information to disseminate about the 2009 Iran presidential elections. On June 12, the race was decided in a landslide for Mahmoud Ahmadinejad over rival Mir Hossein Mousavi. Riots broke out across Iran with charges of voting fraud, and foreign journalists were asked to leave the country. The hash tag (a keyword on Twitter preceded by a "#" that allows for easily searching tweets on a topic) "#iranelection" quickly became a trending topic, and was often the only way to receive information as the country became increasingly closed off to Western reporters. Major news organizations, including CNN, were broadcasting the content of tweets on their website and became increasingly preoccupied with understanding the validity of the information being provided on Twitter.

Other examples of Twitter's use in effectively relaying news occurred when James Karl Buck, an American graduate student who was covering an anti-government protest in Egypt, was arrested on April 10, 2008. He simply twittered the word "Arrested" as he was being escorted to the police station. His tweet was received by his followers and was quickly retweeted (the viral process of repeating a tweet to one's one follower base) drawing attention to his situation that ultimately led to his release. In May 2008, reports of a devastating earthquake in China broke on Twitter before the mainstream media began reporting on it. And news of celebrity deaths, like that of Michael Jackson on June 25, 2009, circulated quickly on Twitter after the website TMZ.com broke the story, long before it was verified by the *Los Angeles Times.*

Whether or not Twitter is a fad or a permanent phenomenon remains to be seen. But these examples point to the value of user-generated content on micro-blogs, the power of repeating that information to your network of followers and the value of real-time search, particularly during breaking news or times of crisis. This offers challenges as well as opportunities for news organizations, which must sift through the avalanche of information and find ways to verify sources and data coming from the community. It offers a way to engage a community of sources that would have never been mobilized in the past. It changes the relationship that the news organization has with its audience from a lecture to a conversation. Organizations can choose to embrace this phenomenon or risk being left behind.

It is still too early to tell which, if any of these innovations will be successful or long term, but these directions are certainly hopeful signs that journalism can and will have a continuing valuable role in society.

DEVELOPING AN EFFECTIVE USER EXPERIENCE

Some news organizations continue to experiment in developing unique and meaningful user experiences, while others are just beginning to consider a foray into this area. While innovation is key, and there are no firm rules, here are some considerations that can help guide the process.

- **Know your audience.** Gather data about online users, local issues and concerns, and pay attention to comments on articles or blogs. Is there an issue of local interest or of broader significant that has a specific local angle? Read other local online publications and pay attention to trends on social media sites. Engage your Twitter followers with questions about potential projects.
- **Play to your competencies/expertise** Focus on the types of projects in which your organization has excelled in the past. Do you have a reporting competency in local politics or crime? Are you in a geographic area where entertainment or sports coverage (like Los Angeles or Las Vegas) has become part of your core operation? Do you have access to unique data sources or archived material and do you have the resources to maintain and update that data, if necessary?
- **Are there existing tools you can leverage?** Have other parts of your organization or external organizations developed a similar project? What can you learn, borrow or purchase from that organization? Can you leverage an external platform, like Twitter, and engage existing applications, or develop new ones with their open-source application programming interface (API)? Or do you need to develop the platform in-house?
- **Do you have development expertise?** An organization must consider the skills necessary to accomplish an interactive project. Do those skills exist in-house? Can they be developed or will your organization need to hire or contract with new resources? Research in the types of technologies used to host will be necessary (for example, is there a platform like Pluck, used by *USA Today* that adds social media features to their publishing system, available for purchase? Will employees need to be trained or hired in web framework technologies like Django or Ruby on Rails in order to develop online interactives? What other perspectives will these employees need to understand in order to develop projects that are both compelling stories and technology tools?

- **How will the user interact with the project?** Navigation, design and usability will be key to the success of any online presentation. Will it be simple, like the *New York Times* WordTrain, that requires the user to input a limited number of items, or will it be more a immersive experience that might require more complex instructions, step-by-step guides or special media players? Are these requirements appropriate to your audience and topic? Use design techniques that will improve the use of the site, including meaningful layout, usage of white space, complementary and contrasting colors and branding, if appropriate. Finally, how will users with sense impairments have access to the materials? An appreciation of accessibility standards will be necessary in engaging as wide an audience as possible. Usability testing should be a standard part of any online project.
- **Be creative.** Encourage creativity amongst your ranks. Have brainstorming sessions or allow employees to peruse the web seeking ideas and inspiration. Look at competitors sites to see the types of projects they are developing, and broaden your definition of competitor to include relevant social media sites, blogs and other technology services. Consider projects that might not initially seem standard on a news website, like the *Washington Post* project "On Being," a video project that provides a quirky, yet poignant take on the fascinating and diverse individuals in their market. Give employees the license to experiment but be ready to accept failure, as long as it is done quickly and cheaply. An experiment using Twitter to crowdsource a story that is unsuccessful may only cost the time of one or few employees, and the learning that comes from such an experience can easily offset the investment. But, a several-thousand-dollar expenditure in new equipment and resources that spans several months or years and ultimately fails is not acceptable or is rarely necessary, given the proliferation of free or relatively inexpensive tools and services available online.

BUSINESS MODELS OF THE FUTURE

As more news organizations begin to understand their role as user-experience creator, thoughts naturally turn to revenue models that might support these activities. The economic downturn of 2009 has caused many publications to cease operation and several continue to struggle under mounting financial pressure and competition. Can effective engagement of social media lead to a profitable business? It is doubtful that one model will emerge that will be the silver bullet to save the industry. However, multiple models can be considered that would be relevant and meaningful to a particular audience. What questions can be asked that could facilitate an understanding of potential business models for the future?

- **What expertise is your organization gaining with these new roles?** Strategies that might be developed into business models include creating interactive web experiences for clients or developing and marketing tools that will assist others in developing online experiences, providing access to data (although privacy concerns would need to be addressed) and managing live, interactive video streams.

- **Seek grants and other types of non-traditional funding.** The *New York Times*, in conjunction with ProPublica, was recently awarded a Knight News Challenge grant to develop DocumentCloud, a tool that will offer an interface that presents and organizes source documents to users. Many new organizations, like the Texas Tribune (texastribune.org) are experimenting with nonprofit models of news delivery.
- **How can information be repurposed on an ongoing basis?** The ability to search, filter and provide meaningful, topic-based archives can continue to drive visitors over time. Consider how content can be aggregated much like the History of Las Vegas project at the *Las Vegas Sun*.
- **What niches can be tapped that can drive subscriptions or higher ad rates?** Can your organization create communities around sports, parenting, local events or issues? What types of merchandise or services can be sold directly to these niches? The book, *The Long Tail*, from *Wired Magazine*'s Chris Anderson, describes a model for motivating sales across a range of niches that are now accessible due to efficiencies of digital delivery and recommendation engines. Niche content could result in higher ad rates for delivering targeted demographics.
- **What can you give away and for what should you expect payment?** In his most recent book, *Free*, Anderson discusses several models that include a free component that may help drive the sales of other products and services. And, in a digital economy, Anderson explains, much more can be "given away," while generating revenue via targeted advertising or, increasingly, upgraded or higher service levels of existing products.
- **How can you measure the success of interactive environments?** Eric Ulken, writing on the Online Journalism Review blog, detailed a number of internal (comments posted, return commenters, times e-mailed, time spent on page) and external (tweets/retweets, Diggs, Delicious saves, inbound links from blogs) metrics employed by *Business Week*. Too often, metrics take the form of hits or page views, but that connotes a mass-media mentality and is restrictive in its relevance. It will be important to understand what people are doing with your content and on your platform and how that translates to influence and ultimately profit. But, it may be a two-step model with long-term benefits. Different metrics may be applicable to measuring different activities for achieving a wide range of goals. And, the value of developing a community or promoting a brand via widespread user engagement may not be immediately quantifiable, but delivers benefits to an organization nonetheless.

There is no single model, like the subscription/ad-based model of the past. There are no easy answers. But, there are models that can provide inspiration in moving forward. News organizations need to look for ways that they can charge a small percentage of their audience that will support the efforts of the entire organization; they need to justify the value of a well-placed ad in a hyperlocal, niche-driven platform; they need to explore relationships with partners that can use their audience as a platform for selling physical goods and services; and they need to understand the value of non-monetary compensation, in engaging in labor exchange or using their platform to promote brand awareness, reputation and community.

And finally, news organizations need to understand that an active user is a desirable user and can create significant value for the organization, as described by Henry Jenkins in *Convergence Culture: Where Old and New Media Collide*. Create an experience that people are passionate about and sell that to advertisers by emphasizing the association with the good feelings of the interaction, like Coca-Cola's presence on *American Idol*. The value is more than just exposure. It is in the way that a user feels about a community in which he actively participates and how that feeling can be transferred to a sponsor. Concert promoters and beer companies have long used this strategy. Associating your product with a popular musician or a live experience about which people are passionate, has value and ultimately drives sales.

The music industry is dealing with the same issues as journalism; an old revenue model that no longer works and an unclear understanding of new models and platforms. But increasingly artists and music companies are realizing that it's all about engaging a fan base and creating a community. It's not easy, and it won't happen overnight, but media organizations already have a head start with decades of experience and the loyalty, although waning, of their audience. These new models require being open to innovation and creativity, but there is much more to be optimistic about than pessimistic, and there are opportunities for more rather than fewer in engaging new models. These suggestions are offered as a starting point for media companies to begin the hard work of soul searching to figure out exactly what they do and to identify their value and unique competencies. Find inspiration in others outside your immediate purview, those in other industries or endeavors. Look to innovative startups and labors of love. Stay abreast of technology breakthroughs and trends by reading publications outside your immediate purview.

CONCLUSION

The news industry will be interested in keeping up with trends in user-generated content. Today's MySpace and Facebook users are gaining the expectation of participation and will expect to engage with media in this way in the future. News organizations will also need to understand how activities on their sites can be aggregated via open standards to social networking profiles as a form of advertising. They will also need to understand ways in which users may employ privacy controls to either display or suppress those activities as it relates to the identities they create and maintain within their communities.

News organizations will also need to understand niche-related business models, a departure from traditional mass media models. Users of social media sites do so within a "long tail" of interests and activities, and it is rare that a single user or a particular piece of content attracts a sizable audience. However, the aggregate of multiple niches is often as large, if not larger, than the mainstream audience. Internet technologies represent a strong opportunity to engage these niches in ways that can generate revenue, demonstrate expertise and/or develop brand awareness, all of which create value.

Social networking trends not only create a sense of urgency for news media to adopt these features, but provide an indication of where competitive endeavors might be emerging. As the news industry struggles to remain relevant and profitable in an online society, it may find solutions and avoid pitfalls by looking at innovative social media companies and the activities of their users. At the heart is a user base that remains engaged and interested in participation. How news organizations interpret this phenomenon may be the salvation of journalism.

SUGGESTED READING

Chung, Deborah. & Kim, Sujin (2008) Blogging activity among cancer patients and their companions: Uses, gratifications, and predictors of outcomes. *Journal of the American Society for Information Science and Technology* 59:2, 297-306.

Diddi, Arvind. & LaRose, Robert (2006) Getting Hooked on News: Uses and Gratifications and the Formation of News Habits Among College Students in an Internet Environment. *Journal of Broadcasting & Electronic Media* 50:2, 193-210.

Ferguson, Douglas, Greer, Clark & Reardon, Michael (2007) Uses and Gratifications of MP3 Players by College Students: Are iPods More Popular than Radio? *Journal of Radio Studies* 14:2, 102-12.

Epilogue

In 1833, Benjamin Day introduced the idea of journalism as mass communication with his penny press phenomenon, the *New York Sun.* Only six years later the poet Henry Wadsworth Longfellow wrote these lines, which are a succinct admonition for those caught up in the turmoil of a new 21st Century communication era:

Look not mournfully into the Past. It comes not back again. Wisely improve the
Present. It is thine. Go forth to meet the shadowy Future without fear …

The goal of the perspectives presented in the chapters of this book is especially to assist in illuminating what presently appears to be the shadowy future of news and quality journalism. Let us go forth.

Contributors

Paul Alonso is a Peruvian author and journalist. He has published three books of fiction in Spanish, and he writes regularly for media in Latin America and the United States. Alonso has a B.A. in Literature from the Pontifical Catholic University of Peru (PUCP), and a dual master's degree in Journalism and Latin American Studies from the University of Texas at Austin, where he currently is a Ph.D. student in Journalism. His research focuses on the convergence of journalism, entertainment and popular culture. Other research interests include journalism in Latin America, the satirical press, and media and culture. He has worked for the Knight Center for Journalism in the Americas since 2004.

Brian Baresch has been a working journalist for more than 20 years, most of which was spent on copy desks at various newspapers. He has also edited for book, magazine and online publishers, and continues that work while he finishes his doctorate in Journalism at the University of Texas. He is studying the deep effects of cultural narratives on the daily news and trying to discover and understand the various strategies we use to stay informed in the perpetually changing worlds of old and new media. He believes Jon Stewart is this era's leading media critic.

David D. Brown is executive producer and host of the award-winning cultural journalism program "Texas Music Matters" at Austin NPR affiliate KUT-FM. He is former anchor of the Peabody Award-winning public radio business program "Marketplace" and a veteran public radio journalist. He has reported national and international affairs for NPR and PRI's Monitor Radio from bases in Atlanta, Boston, London, Los Angeles, and Washington, D.C. Brown is currently completing his Ph.D. in Journalism at the University of Texas at Austin, and has been an active member of the California Bar since 2000.

Amber Willard Hinsley worked as a newspaper reporter and editor in Los Angeles before beginning her doctoral studies at the University of Texas at Austin. Much of her research has been drawn from her experiences as a journalist, including the renegotiation of news workers' identities as they navigate the sea change sweeping the industry today. She also conducts research on the intersections of psychology and social media use. She has an M.S. in Journalism & Mass Communications from Kansas State University and a B.A. in Communication-Journalism from Truman State University.

Kelly Kaufhold enjoyed a 20-year broadcast and print journalism career in Ohio, Texas and Florida before being accepted to the Ph.D. program in Journalism at the University of Texas at Austin. He has also taught public affairs, radio and television reporting. His diverse research revolves around young adults, news and informed democracy, and how they are influenced by political communication and digital media. Kelly's academic studies have examined the role of age in news judgment, comparisons of traditional versus new media on knowledge and participation, and the perspectives of community newspaper editors on citizen journalism.

Dominic Lasorsa (Ph.D., Stanford University) is an associate professor in the School of Journalism at the University of Texas at Austin, where he studies political communication, new media, and media effects. Lasorsa's work has appeared in *the Encyclopedia of International Media and Communications, The Historical Dictionary of Political Communication in the United States, The International Journal of Public Opinion Research, The Journal of Communication, The Journal of Media Economics, The Journal of Reading, Journalism and Mass Communication Quarterly, Journalism Practice, Journalism Studies, Newspaper Research Journal,* and *Writer's Digest.* He was co-author of the three-volume *National Television Violence Study* (1996-98) and *How to Build Social Science Theories* (2004).

Jaime Loke is a Ph.D. student in the School of Journalism at the University of Texas at Austin. She has a B.A. in journalism and English from Indiana University (Bloomington) and an M.A. in journalism from the University of Texas. Her research considers the various intersections of gender constructions in the media, the critical and cultural perspectives of gender issues in mass communication, and the emerging new public spaces in the online sphere.

Seth C. Lewis is a Ph.D. candidate in the School of Journalism and the Mike Hogg Fellow at the University of Texas at Austin. A former editor at *The Miami Herald*, he studies digital media work and culture, with an emphasis on innovation in journalism. His research has appeared in peer-reviewed journals including *Journalism & Mass Communication Quarterly, Journalism, Journalism Studies, Journalism Practice,* and *Newspaper Research Journal.* Lewis holds an MBA from Barry University and a B.A. in communication from Brigham Young University, and in 2005 he was a Fulbright Scholar to Spain. For more information, visit www.sethlewis.org.

Maxwell McCombs (Ph.D., Stanford University) is the Jesse H. Jones Centennial Chair in Communication at the University of Texas at Austin. Dr. McCombs is internationally recognized for his research on the agenda-setting role of mass communication, the influence of the media on the focus of public attention. Since the original Chapel Hill study with his colleague Donald Shaw coined the term "agenda setting" in 1968, more than 400 studies of agenda setting have been conducted worldwide.

McCombs' most recent book, *Setting the Agenda: The Mass Media and Public Opinion*, was published in 2004 and has been translated into Spanish, Chinese, Polish, and Swedish. He is a past president of the World Association for Public Opinion Research and a fellow of the International Communication Association. In his early career, he was a reporter for the *New Orleans Times-Picayune*.

Cindy Royal (Ph.D., University of Texas at Austin) is an assistant professor in the School of Journalism and Mass Communication at Texas State University in San Marcos. At the University of Texas, her research focused on the effects of the Internet on communication and culture. At Texas State, she teaches Web Design and other online media courses. Prior to doctoral studies, Dr. Royal had a career in marketing at Compaq Computer (now part of Hewlett-Packard) in Houston and NCR Corporation in Dayton, Ohio. She has an MBA from the University of Richmond and a B.S. in business administration from the University of North Carolina at Chapel Hill. Additional details regarding her research, education, and experience can be found at www.cindyroyal.com. She hosts a music blog at www.onthatnote.com and a tech blog at www.cindytech.wordpress.com.

Amy Schmitz Weiss (Ph.D., University of Texas at Austin) is an assistant professor in the School of Journalism and Media Studies at San Diego State University. She was a co-founder of her college online newspaper and has worked at Chicago Tribune Online and Indianapolis Star News Online, where she produced and wrote news packages. Schmitz Weiss has also worked in business development, marketing analysis, and account management for several Chicago Internet media firms. Her research interests include online journalism, media sociology, news production, multimedia journalism, and international communication. She has an M.A. in Journalism from the University of Texas at Austin and a B.A. in Journalism and Spanish from Butler University.

LaVergne, TN USA
19 January 2010
170407LV00001B/1/P